Best in the World

175 classic recipes from the great cuisines

Best in the World

175 classic recipes from the great cuisines

From Italy and Thailand to Russia, India and Japan – original food and cooking from around the globe featured in easy-to-follow recipes and 200 step-by-step colour photographs

Martha Day

southwater

This edition is published by Southwater, an imprint of Anness Publishing Ltd,
Hermes House, 88–89 Blackfriars Road, London SE1 8HA
tel. 020 7401 2077; fax 020 7633 9499

www.southwaterbooks.com; www.annesspublishing.com

If you like the images in this book and would like to investigate using them for
publishing, promotions or advertising, please visit our website
www.practicalpictures.com for more information.

UK agent: The Manning Partnership Ltd
tel. 01225 478444; fax 01225 478440; sales@manning-partnership.co.uk
UK distributor: Grantham Book Services Ltd
tel. 01476 541080; fax 01476 541061; orders@gbs.tbs-ltd.co.uk
North American agent/distributor: National Book Network
tel. 301 459 3366; fax 301 429 5746; www.nbnbooks.com
Australian agent/distributor: Pan Macmillan Australia
tel. 1300 135 113; fax 1300 135 103; customer.service@macmillan.com.au
New Zealand agent/distributor: David Bateman Ltd
tel. (09) 415 7664; fax (09) 415 8892

Publisher: Joanna Lorenz
Senior Managing Editor: Conor Kilgallon
Editor: Elizabeth Woodland
Production Controller: Wendy Lawson
Design: SMI
Photographers: Karl Adamson, Edward Allwright, Steve Baxter, James Duncan,
Michelle Garrett, Amanda Heywood, Don Last, Patrick McLeavy, Michael Michaels
Additional photography: Sopexa UK
Recipes: Carla Capalbo, Maxine Clark, Frances Cleary, Carole Clements, Roz
Denny, Christine France, Sarah Gates, Shirley Gill, Rosamund Grant, Sue Maggs,
Annie Nichols, Jenny Stacey, Liz Trigg, Hilaire Walden, Laura Washburn, Steven
Wheeler, Elizabeth Wolf-Cohen
Food for Photography: Joanne Craig, Wendy Lee, Jenny Shapter, Jane Stevenson,
Elizabeth Wolf-Cohen
Home Economists: Carla Capalbo, Jenny Shapter
Stylists: Madeleine Brehaut, Carla Capalbo, Michelle Garrett, Hilary Guy, Amanda
Heywood, Blake Minton, Kirsty Rawlings, Rebecca Sturrock, Fiona Tillett

© Anness Publishing Ltd 2007

Previously published as part of a larger volume, 500 Best-Ever Recipes

Ethical Trading Policy

At Anness Publishing we believe that business should be conducted in an ethical
and ecologically sustainable way, with respect for the environment and a proper
regard to the replacement of the natural resources we employ.

As a publisher, we use a lot of wood pulp to make high-quality paper for
printing, and that wood commonly comes from spruce trees. We are therefore
currently growing more than 500,000 trees in two Scottish forest plantations
near Aberdeen – Berrymoss (130 hectares/320 acres) and West Touxhill (125
hectares/305 acres). The forests we manage contain twice the number of trees
employed each year in paper-making for our books.

Because of this ongoing ecological investment programme, you, as our
customer, can have the pleasure and reassurance of knowing that a tree is being
cultivated on your behalf to naturally replace the materials used to make the
book you are holding.

Our forestry programme is run in accordance with the UK Woodland
Assurance Scheme (UKWAS) and will be certified by the internationally
recognized Forest Stewardship Council (FSC). The FSC is a non-government
organization dedicated to promoting responsible management of the world's
forests. Certification ensures forests are managed in an environmentally
sustainable and socially responsible basis. For further information about this
scheme, go to www.annesspublishing.com/trees

Notes

Bracketed terms are intended for American readers.
For all recipes, quantities are given in both metric and imperial measures and,
where appropriate, in standard cups and spoons. Follow one set, but not a
mixture, because they are not interchangeable.
Standard spoon and cup measures are level. 1 tsp = 5ml, 1 tbsp = 15ml,
1 cup = 250ml/8fl oz.
Australian standard tablespoons are 20ml. Australian readers should use 3 tsp in
place of 1 tbsp for measuring small quantities of gelatine, flour, salt etc.
American pints are 16fl oz/2 cups. American readers should use 20fl oz/2½ cups
in place of 1 pint when measuring liquids.
Electric oven temperatures in this book are for conventional ovens. When using
a fan oven, the temperature will probably need to be reduced by about
10–20°C/20–40°F. Since ovens vary, you should check with your manufacturer's
instruction book for guidance.
The nutritional analysis given for each recipe is calculated per portion
(i.e. serving or item), unless otherwise stated. If the recipe gives a range,
such as Serves 4–6, then the nutritional analysis will be for the smaller
portion size, i.e. serves 6.
Medium (US large) eggs are used unless otherwise stated.

Cover illustrations
Front cover, clockwise from top: Pepperoni Pizza p71; Dim Sum, p15;
Spanish Seafood Paella, p37; Lasagne, p70; Sushi, p16; Pot-Roast Poussin, p55.

Contents

Introduction

In the modern world's quest for innovation and new taste sensations, it's easy to forget just how delicious and fulfilling a classic recipe can be. This volume contains an exhaustive selection of best-ever recipes from around the world.

These cosmopolitan creations have gained world-wide status through their harmonious balance of fresh ingredients, herbs and spices. Justifiably popular in their homelands, they have since attained universal appeal as part of the international chef's repertoire. Even more appealing is that many of these recipes are healthy too, and nutritional information is given for each one to help you plan and maintain a low-fat eating programme.

The dishes in this book are tailored to every season and every event: you can mix and match cooking styles and influences to suit the mood and the occasion, not to mention your pocket. There is a fine selection of hearty soups such as French Onion Soup and New England Pumpkin soup, which both make an attractive and delicious first course. Or try one of the sophisticated appetizers such as Chicken Liver Pâté with Marsala, Grilled Garlic Mussels or a fresh Classic Greek Salad.

Fish and shellfish are increasingly popular in today's health-conscious society. Flavoursome taste sensations such as Middle Eastern Sea Bream or Moroccan Fish Tagine are delightful dishes that will tantalize your tastebuds.

This volume also includes a variety of the best and most celebrated meat dishes from around the world, and shows how simple it can be to present the perfect Roast Beef with

Yorkshire Pudding or some mouth-tingling spicy Indian Curried Lamb Samosas. Whilst many are long-standing favourites, such as Chicken Stroganoff, others are authentic versions of more unusual world-famous dishes, such as Hungarian Beef Goulash and Mandarin Sesame Duck, which combine a rich, colourful appearance with satisfying textures and harmonious flavours.

There are also more unusual dishes, such as Moroccan Chicken Couscous – a simple yet impressive dinner party offering, and economical yet nutritious suggestions that will appeal to adults and children alike, such as Best-ever American Burgers, Corned Beef and Egg Hash, and Middle-Eastern Lamb Kebabs. Whether you choose western fare such as Tuna Fishcake Bites, Pepperoni Pizza or an exotic Kashmir Coconut Fish Curry, the recipes are characterized by a distinctive depth of flavour created by a judicious blend of herbs and spices.

The vegetable dishes in this book are tempting concoctions for both accompaniments and for complete, well-balanced meals. There are many appetizing vegetarian choices to choose from, including a hearty Middle-Eastern Vegetable Stew, a simple Avocado and Tomato Salad, and scrumptious Greek Spinach and Cheese Pies.

To finish, the moment that many have been waiting for: the dessert course. These range from super-smooth ice creams to the richest trifles, and dreamy desserts made from fruit, cream and chocolate. End the meal on a high note with family favourites such as Crème Caramel and Baked American Cheesecake, or why not try something more exotic like Thai Fried Bananas?

This marvellous collection of recipes has been drawn together from the combined talents of some of the world's most respected cooks and food writers, and with this authoritative kitchen guide to hand, you are sure to find the perfect dish for any occasion.

Minestrone with Pesto

This hearty, Italian mixed vegetable soup is a great way to use up any leftover vegetables you may have.

Serves 4
30ml/2 tbsp olive oil
2 garlic cloves, crushed
1 onion, sliced
225g/8oz/2 cups diced lean bacon
2 small courgettes (zucchini),
    quartered and sliced
50g/2oz/1½ cups green
    beans, chopped
2 small carrots, diced
2 celery sticks, finely chopped
1 bouquet garni

50g/2oz/½ cup short-cut
    macaroni or other soup pasta
50g/2oz/½ cup frozen peas
200g/7oz can red kidney beans,
    drained and rinsed
50g/2oz/1 cup shredded
    green cabbage
4 tomatoes, peeled and seeded
salt and ground black pepper
basil, to garnish (optional)

For the toasts
8 slices French bread
15ml/1 tbsp ready-made
    pesto sauce
15ml/1 tbsp freshly grated
    Parmesan cheese

1 Heat the oil in a large pan over low heat. Add the garlic and onion and cook, stirring occasionally, for 5 minutes, until just softened but not coloured.

2 Add the bacon, courgettes, green beans, carrots and celery to the pan and stir-fry for a further 3 minutes.

3 Pour 1.2 litres/2 pints/5 cups water over the vegetables and add the bouquet garni. Cover the pan with a tight-fitting lid and simmer for 25 minutes.

4 Add the macaroni, peas and kidney beans and cook for a further 8 minutes. Then add the cabbage and tomatoes and cook for 5 minutes more, until all the vegetables and the pasta are tender.

5 To make the toasts, spread the bread slices with the pesto, sprinkle a little Parmesan over each one and gently brown under a hot grill (broiler). Remove and discard the bouquet garni from the soup, season to taste and serve with the toasts.

French Onion Soup

Onion soup comes in many different guises from light, smooth and creamy to this rich, dark brown version – the absolute classic recipe from France.

Serves 4
25g/1oz/2 tbsp butter
15ml/1 tbsp sunflower oil
3 large onions, thinly sliced
5ml/1 tsp soft dark brown sugar
15g/½ oz/1 tbsp plain (all-
    purpose) flour

2 x 300g/10oz cans condensed
    beef consommé
30ml/2 tbsp medium sherry
10ml/2 tsp Worcestershire sauce
8 slices French bread
15ml/1 tbsp French coarse-
    grained mustard
75g/3oz Gruyère cheese, grated
salt and ground black pepper
15ml/1 tbsp chopped fresh flat
    leaf parsley, to garnish

1 Heat the butter and oil in a large pan over low heat. Add the onions and brown sugar and cook gently, stirring occasionally, for at least 20 minutes, until the onions start to turn golden brown and caramelize. (Depending on the variety, you may need to cook them for longer.)

2 Stir in the flour and cook, stirring constantly, for a further 2 minutes. Pour in the consommé and stir in two cans of water, then add the sherry and Worcestershire sauce. Season with salt and pepper, cover the pan with a tight-fitting lid and simmer gently for a further 25–30 minutes.

3 Preheat the grill (broiler) and, just before you are ready to serve, toast the bread lightly on both sides. Spread one side of each slice with the mustard and top with the grated cheese. Grill (broil) the toasts until the cheese has melted and is bubbling and golden.

4 Ladle the soup into warmed soup bowls. Place two slices of toasted bread on top of each bowl of soup and sprinkle with chopped fresh parsley to garnish. Alternatively, place the toasted bread in the base of the bowls and ladle the soup over them, then garnish with the parsley. Serve immediately.

Minestrone Energy 570kcal/2396kJ; Protein 26.9g; Carbohydrate 72.8g, of which sugars 12.5g; Fat 21g, of which saturates 6g; Cholesterol 35mg; Calcium 247mg; Fibre 9g; Sodium 1635mg.
Onion Energy 415kcal/1745kJ; Protein 13g; Carbohydrate 61.6g, of which sugars 12.6g; Fat 14.1g, of which saturates 6.7g; Cholesterol 25mg; Calcium 240mg; Fibre 4.1g; Sodium 1022mg.

New England Pumpkin Soup

For a smooth-textured soup, process all the mixture in a food processor or blender.

Serves 4
25g/1oz/2 tbsp butter
1 onion, finely chopped
1 garlic clove, crushed
15g/½ oz/1 tbsp plain (all-purpose) flour
pinch of grated nutmeg
2.5ml/½ tsp ground cinnamon
350g/12oz pumpkin, seeded, peeled and diced

600ml/1 pint/2½ cups chicken stock
150ml/¼ pint/⅔ cup freshly squeezed orange juice
5ml/1 tsp brown sugar

For the croûtons
15ml/1 tbsp vegetable oil
2 slices multigrain bread, crusts removed
30ml/2 tbsp sunflower seeds
salt and ground black pepper

1 Melt the butter in a large pan over low heat. Add the onion and garlic and cook, stirring occasionally, for 4–5 minutes, until softened but not coloured.

2 Stir in the flour, nutmeg, cinnamon and pumpkin, then cover the pan and cook gently, stirring occasionally, for 6 minutes.

3 Add the chicken stock, orange juice and brown sugar. Cover the pan again, and bring to the boil, then simmer for 20 minutes until the pumpkin has softened.

4 Leave to cool slightly, then ladle half the mixture into a blender or food processor and process until smooth. Return the soup to the pan with the remaining chunky mixture. Season to taste and heat through, stirring constantly.

5 To make the croûtons, heat the oil in a frying pan, cut the bread into cubes and gently fry until just beginning to brown. Add the sunflower seeds and fry for 1–2 minutes. Drain the croûtons on kitchen paper. Serve the soup hot, garnished with a few of the croûtons sprinkled over the top and the remaining croûtons separately.

Thai-style Chicken Soup

Like most Thai soups this one is quick and easy to prepare and may be served as a first course, a snack or a light lunch.

Serves 4
15ml/1 tbsp vegetable oil
1 garlic clove, finely chopped
2 x 175g/6oz boned chicken breast portions, skinned and chopped
2.5ml/½ tsp ground turmeric
1.5ml/¼ tsp hot chilli powder
75ml/5 tbsp coconut cream
900ml/1½ pints/3¾ cups hot chicken stock

30ml/2 tbsp lemon or lime juice
30ml/2 tbsp crunchy peanut butter
50g/2oz thread egg noodles, broken into small pieces
15ml/1 tbsp finely chopped spring onions (scallions)
15ml/1 tbsp chopped fresh coriander (cilantro)
salt and ground black pepper
30ml/2 tbsp desiccated (dry unsweetened shredded) coconut and ½ red chilli, seeded and finely chopped, to garnish

1 Heat the oil in a large, heavy pan over medium heat. Add the garlic and stir-fry for 1 minute, until lightly golden. Add the chicken, turmeric and chilli powder and stir-fry for a further 3–4 minutes.

2 Mix together the coconut cream and chicken stock until thoroughly combined and pour into the pan. Add the lemon or lime juice, peanut butter and egg noodles and bring to the boil, stirring constantly. Lower the heat, cover and simmer gently for 15 minutes

3 Add the spring onions and coriander, season to taste with salt and pepper and cook for a further 5 minutes.

4 Meanwhile, heat a small frying pan, add the coconut and chilli and dry-fry, stirring constantly, for 2–3 minutes, until the coconut is lightly browned.

5 Ladle the soup into warmed soup bowls and sprinkle the coconut and chilli garnish over each. Serve immediately.

Thai Chicken Soup Energy 342kcal/1425kJ; Protein 25.7g; Carbohydrate 11.6g, of which sugars 2.4g; Fat 21.7g, of which saturates 13g; Cholesterol 65mg; Calcium 40mg; Fibre 1.4g; Sodium 111mg.
Pumpkin Soup Energy 189kcal/788kJ; Protein 4.1g; Carbohydrate 17.1g, of which sugars 6.4g; Fat 12.1g, of which saturates 4.1g; Cholesterol 13mg; Calcium 76mg; Fibre 2.2g; Sodium 109mg.

Scotch Broth

Sustaining and warming, this traditional Scottish soup makes a delicious winter dish anywhere in the world.

Serves 6–8
900g/2lb lean neck (US shoulder) of lamb, cut into large even-size chunks
1.75 litres/3 pints/7½ cups water

1 large onion, chopped
50g/2oz/¼ cup pearl barley
1 bouquet garni
1 large carrot, chopped
1 turnip, chopped
3 leeks, chopped
½ small white cabbage, shredded
salt and ground black pepper
chopped fresh parsley, to garnish

1 Put the lamb and measured water into a large pan and bring to the boil over medium heat. Skim off the scum, then stir in the onion, barley and bouquet garni.

2 Bring the soup back to the boil, lower the heat, partly cover the pan and simmer gently for 1 hour.

3 Add the carrot, turnip, leeks and cabbage and season to taste with salt and pepper. Bring back to the boil, partly cover the pan again and simmer gently for about 35 minutes, until the vegetables are tender.

4 Remove and discard any surplus fat that has risen to the top of the soup, then ladle into warmed soup bowls, sprinkle with chopped parsley and serve immediately.

Cook's Tip
Lamb stock is too strongly flavoured for general use but ideal for making this soup. Put 1.3kg/3lb shoulder and/or breast bones of lamb into a large pan, add 2.75 litres/5 pints/11½ cups water and bring to the boil. Skim off the scum, then lower the heat and simmer for 45 minutes. Skim again and add 2 coarsely chopped carrots, 2 coarsely chopped onions, 1 bouquet garni, 1 bay leaf and 6 black peppercorns. Simmer for a further 2 hours, then strain and chill.

Split Pea & Courgette Soup

Rich and satisfying, this tasty and nutritious soup is ideal to serve on a chilly winter's day. Served with crusty bread it's perfect for lunch.

Serves 4
175g/6oz/1 cup yellow split peas
5ml/1 tsp sunflower oil

1 large onion, finely chopped
2 courgettes (zucchini), finely diced
900ml/1½ pints/3¾ cups chicken stock
2.5ml/½ tsp ground turmeric
salt and ground black pepper
warm crusty bread, to serve

1 Place the split peas in a bowl, cover with cold water and leave to soak for several hours or overnight. Drain, rinse in cold water and drain again.

2 Heat the oil in a pan over low heat. Add the onion, cover the pan with a tight-fitting lid and cook for about 8 minutes, until softened but not coloured.

3 Reserve a handful of diced courgettes and add the remainder to the pan. Increase the heat to medium and cook, stirring constantly, for 2–3 minutes.

4 Add the chicken stock and turmeric to the pan and bring to the boil. Reduce the heat to low, cover and simmer gently for 30–40 minutes, or until the split peas are tender. Season to taste with salt and pepper.

5 When the soup is almost ready, bring a large pan of water to the boil, add the reserved diced courgettes and cook for 1 minute, then drain and add to the soup before serving hot with warm crusty bread.

Cook's Tip
For a quicker alternative, use split red lentils for this soup. They do not require presoaking and cook very quickly. Adjust the amount of chicken stock used, if you need to.

Scotch Broth Energy 267kcal/1118kJ; Protein 24.7g; Carbohydrate 12.9g, of which sugars 6.2g; Fat 13.3g, of which saturates 5.9g; Cholesterol 86mg; Calcium 58mg; Fibre 3.2g; Sodium 106mg.
Split Pea Energy 182kcal/769kJ; Protein 12.2g; Carbohydrate 31.5g, of which sugars 6.1g; Fat 1.7g, of which saturates 0.2g; Cholesterol 0mg; Calcium 54mg; Fibre 3.7g; Sodium 19mg.

Smoked Haddock Pâté

This easily prepared pâté is made with Arbroath Smokies, small haddock which have been salted and hot-smoked.

Serves 6

butter, for greasing
3 large Arbroath Smokies (about 225g/8oz each) or other smoked haddock
275g/10oz/1¼ cups medium-fat soft (farmer's) cheese
3 eggs, lightly beaten
30–45ml/2–3 tbsp lemon juice
ground black pepper
fresh chervil sprigs, to garnish
lemon wedges and lettuce leaves, to serve

1 Preheat the oven to 160°C/325°F/Gas 3. Generously grease six individual ramekins with butter.

2 Place the fish in an ovenproof dish and heat through in the oven for 10 minutes. Carefully remove and discard the skin and bones from the fish, then flake the flesh into a bowl.

3 Mash the fish with a fork and gradually work in the cheese, then the eggs. Add the lemon juice and season with black pepper to taste.

4 Divide the fish mixture among the six ramekins and place in a roasting pan. Pour hot water into the roasting pan to come about halfway up the sides of the dishes. Bake for 30 minutes, until just set.

5 Leave to cool for 2–3 minutes, then run a knife point around the edge of each dish and invert on to a warmed plate. Garnish with fresh chervil sprigs and serve immediately with the lemon wedges and lettuce.

> **Variation**
> This pâté is also tasty made with hot-smoked trout fillets. You can then omit the initial cooking in step 2.

Spinach, Bacon & Prawn Salad

Serve this hot salad with plenty of crusty bread to mop up the delicious juices.

Serves 4

105ml/7 tbsp olive oil
30ml/2 tbsp sherry vinegar
2 garlic cloves, finely chopped
5ml/1 tsp Dijon mustard
12 cooked king prawns (jumbo shrimp), in the shell
115g/4oz rindless streaky (fatty) bacon, cut into strips
115g/4oz/2 cups fresh young spinach leaves
½ head oak leaf lettuce, coarsely torn
salt and ground black pepper

1 To make the dressing, whisk together 90ml/6 tbsp of the olive oil with the vinegar, garlic and mustard in a small pan and season to taste with salt and pepper. Heat gently, whisking constantly, until slightly thickened, then remove from the heat and keep warm.

2 Carefully remove the heads and peel the prawns, leaving their tails intact. Cut along the back of each prawn and remove the dark vein. Set the prawns aside until needed.

3 Heat the remaining oil in a frying pan over medium heat. Add the bacon and cook, stirring occasionally, until golden and crisp. Add the prawns and stir-fry for a few minutes until warmed through.

4 Meanwhile, arrange the spinach leaves and lettuce leaves on four individual serving plates.

5 Spoon the bacon and prawns on to the leaves, then pour the hot dressing over them. Serve immediately.

> **Cook's Tip**
> Sherry vinegar lends its pungent, nutty flavour to this delicious salad. It is readily available in large supermarkets or delicatessens. However, ordinary red or white wine vinegar could be used instead if you like.

Pâté Energy 253kcal/1049kJ; Protein 17.9g; Carbohydrate 1.4g, of which sugars 1.4g; Fat 19.6g, of which saturates 6.6g; Cholesterol 151mg; Calcium 46mg; Fibre 0g; Sodium 527mg.
Salad Energy 320kcal/1325kJ; Protein 18.8g; Carbohydrate 0.9g, of which sugars 0.9g; Fat 26.8g, of which saturates 5.3g; Cholesterol 165mg; Calcium 117mg; Fibre 0.8g; Sodium 546mg.

Chicken Liver Pâté with Marsala

This is a really quick and simple pâté to make, yet it has a delicious – and quite sophisticated – flavour.

Serves 4

350g/12oz chicken livers, thawed
   if frozen
225g/8oz/1 cup butter
2 garlic cloves, crushed
15ml/1 tbsp Marsala
5ml/1 tsp chopped sage
salt and ground black pepper
8 fresh sage leaves, to garnish
Melba toast, to serve

1 Pick over the chicken livers, then rinse and pat dry with kitchen paper. Melt 25g/1oz/2 tbsp of the butter in a frying pan over medium heat. Add the chicken livers and garlic and cook, stirring occasionally, for about 5 minutes, or until they are firm but still pink in their centres.

2 Transfer the livers to a food processor or blender using a slotted spoon. Add the Marsala and chopped sage.

3 Melt 150g/5oz/generous ½ cup of the remaining butter in the frying pan, stirring to loosen any sediment, then pour into the food processor or blender and process until smooth. Season well with salt and pepper.

4 Spoon the pâté into four individual pots and smooth the surface. Melt the remaining butter in a separate pan and pour it over the pâtés. Garnish with sage leaves and chill in the refrigerator until set. Serve with triangles of Melba toast.

Cook's Tip
To make Melba toast, first remove the crusts from medium-sliced white bread. Toast on both sides in a toaster or under the grill (broiler), until golden. Remove the toast and, using a sharp, serrated knife, cut horizontally through each slice to make two very thin slices. Cut each slice into quarters and toast the uncooked sides under the grill until golden and curling. Cool on a rack and store in an airtight container.

Salmon Rillettes

A variation on the classic French pork rillette, this appetizer is easier and less time consuming to make than the original.

Serves 6

350g/12oz salmon fillets
175g/6oz/¾ cup butter
1 leek, white part only,
   finely chopped
1 celery stick, finely chopped
1 bay leaf
150ml/¼ pint/⅔ cup dry
   white wine
115g/4oz smoked
   salmon trimmings
large pinch of ground mace
60ml/4 tbsp fromage frais
   (low-fat cream cheese)
salt and ground black pepper
salad leaves, to serve

1 Lightly season the salmon with salt and pepper. Melt 25g/1oz/2 tbsp of the butter in a frying pan over low heat. Add the celery and leek and cook, stirring occasionally, for about 5 minutes. Add the salmon and bay leaf and pour in the wine. Cover with a tight-fitting lid and cook for about 15 minutes, until the fish is tender. Set the salmon aside.

2 Strain the cooking liquid into another pan, bring to the boil and cook until reduced to 30ml/2 tbsp. Leave to cool.

3 Melt 50g/2oz/4 tbsp of the remaining butter in another pan and gently cook the smoked salmon until it turns pale pink. Leave to cool.

4 Remove the skin and any bones from the salmon fillets. Flake the flesh into a bowl and add the reduced cooking liquid. Beat in the remaining butter, the mace and fromage frais. Break up the smoked salmon trimmings and fold into the mixture with the pan juices. Taste and adjust the seasoning.

5 Spoon the salmon mixture into a dish or terrine and smooth the surface. Cover and chill in the refrigerator.

6 To serve the salmon rillettes, shape the mixture into oval quenelles using two dessert spoons and arrange on individual plates with the salad leaves.

Chicken Energy 507kcal/2090kJ; Protein 16g; Carbohydrate 1g, of which sugars 0.6g; Fat 48.3g, of which saturates 29.9g; Cholesterol 452mg; Calcium 18mg; Fibre 0.1g; Sodium 408mg.
Salmon Energy 373kcal/1542kJ; Protein 17.4g; Carbohydrate 1.2g, of which sugars 1g; Fat 31.4g, of which saturates 16.5g; Cholesterol 98mg; Calcium 33mg; Fibre 0.7g; Sodium 568mg.

Spinach & Cheese Dumplings

These tasty little dumplings are known as *gnocchi* in Italy, where they are extremely popular, especially in the northern regions.

Serves 4
butter, for greasing
40g/1½oz/½ cup freshly grated Parmesan cheese
175g/6oz cold mashed potato
75g/3oz/½ cup semolina
115g/4oz/1 cup frozen leaf spinach, thawed, squeezed out and chopped
115g/4oz/½ cup ricotta cheese
30ml/2 tbsp beaten egg
2.5ml/½ tsp salt
large pinch of grated nutmeg
pinch of ground black pepper
fresh basil sprigs, to garnish

For the butter sauce
75g/3oz/6 tbsp butter
5ml/1 tsp grated lemon rind
15ml/1 tbsp lemon juice
15ml/1 tbsp chopped fresh basil

1 Preheat the oven to 150°C/300°F/Gas 2. Lightly grease a flameproof dish with butter and place it in the oven to warm. Set aside 30ml/2 tbsp of the Parmesan cheese. Place the remainder in a bowl, add the potato, semolina, spinach, ricotta, beaten egg, salt, nutmeg and pepper and mix well.

2 Take walnut-size pieces of the mixture and roll each one back and forth along the prongs of a fork until ridged. Make 28 dumplings in this way. Preheat the grill (broiler).

3 Bring a large pan of water to the boil, reduce to a simmer and drop in the dumplings. As they cook they will rise to the surface; this takes about 2 minutes, then simmer for 1 minute more. Transfer the dumplings to the prepared dish.

4 Sprinkle the dumplings with the Parmesan cheese and grill under high heat for 2 minutes, or until lightly browned.

5 Meanwhile, heat the butter in a pan and stir in the lemon rind, lemon juice and basil. Season to taste with salt and pepper. Pour some of this butter over each portion and serve immediately, garnished with basil sprigs.

Kansas City Fritters

Crisp bacon and vegetable fritters are served with a spicy tomato salsa.

Makes 8
200g/7oz/1¾ cups canned corn, drained well
2 eggs, separated
75g/3oz/¾ cup plain (all-purpose) flour
75ml/5 tbsp milk
1 small courgette (zucchini), grated
2 rashers (strips) rindless lean back bacon, diced
2 spring onions (scallions), finely chopped
large pinch of cayenne pepper
45ml/3 tbsp sunflower oil
salt and ground black pepper
fresh coriander (cilantro) sprigs, to garnish

For the salsa
3 tomatoes, peeled, seeded and diced
½ small red (bell) pepper, seeded and diced
½ small onion, diced
15ml/1 tbsp lemon juice
15ml/1 tbsp chopped fresh coriander
dash of Tabasco sauce

1 To make the salsa, mix all the ingredients together in a bowl and season to taste with salt and pepper. Cover with clear film (plastic wrap) and chill until required.

2 Empty the corn into another bowl and mix in the egg yolks. Add the flour and blend in with a wooden spoon. When the mixture thickens, gradually blend in the milk.

3 Stir in the courgette, bacon, spring onions and cayenne pepper and season with salt and pepper. Whisk the egg whites in a grease-free bowl until stiff peaks form. Gently fold into the corn batter mixture.

4 Heat the oil in a large frying pan and place four spoonfuls of the mixture into it. Cook over a medium heat for 2–3 minutes on each side, until golden. Drain on kitchen paper and keep warm in the oven while cooking the remaining four fritters.

5 Serve two fritters each, garnished with coriander sprigs and a spoonful of the chilled tomato salsa.

Fritters Energy 152kcal/636kJ; Protein 5.3g; Carbohydrate 17.2g, of which sugars 5.6g; Fat 7.4g, of which saturates 1.5g; Cholesterol 51mg; Calcium 42mg; Fibre 1.5g; Sodium 190mg.
Dumplings Energy 432kcal/1796kJ; Protein 18.2g; Carbohydrate 23.1g, of which sugars 2g; Fat 30.3g, of which saturates 18.2g; Cholesterol 126mg; Calcium 381mg; Fibre 1.4g; Sodium 465mg.

Grilled Garlic Mussels

Use a combination of fresh herbs, such as oregano, basil and flat leaf parsley.

Serves 4

1.5kg/3–3½lb fresh mussels
120ml/4fl oz/½ cup dry
   white wine
50g/2oz/4 tbsp butter
2 shallots, finely chopped
2 garlic cloves, crushed
50g/2oz/½ cup dried
   white breadcrumbs
60ml/4 tbsp mixed chopped
   fresh herbs
30ml/2 tbsp freshly grated
   Parmesan cheese
salt and ground black pepper
fresh basil leaves, to garnish

1 Scrub the mussels well under cold running water. Remove the "beards" and discard any mussels with damaged shells or that do not shut immediately when sharply tapped.

2 Place in a large, heavy pan with the wine. Cover with a tight-fitting lid and cook over high heat, shaking the pan occasionally for 5–8 minutes, until the mussels have opened.

3 Strain the mussels and reserve the cooking liquid. Discard any mussels that remain closed. Leave them to cool slightly, then remove and discard the top half of each shell.

4 Melt the butter in a pan over low heat. Add the shallots and cook, stirring occasionally, for 5 minutes, until softened. Add the garlic and cook for 1–2 minutes. Add the breadcrumbs and cook, stirring until lightly browned. Remove the pan from the heat and stir in the herbs. Moisten with a little of the reserved mussel liquid, then season to taste with salt and pepper.

5 Spoon the breadcrumb mixture over the mussels and arrange on baking sheets. Sprinkle with the grated Parmesan.

6 Cook the mussels under a hot grill (broiler), in batches, for about 2 minutes, until the topping is crisp and golden brown. Keep the cooked mussels warm in a low oven while grilling (broiling) the remainder. Garnish with fresh basil leaves and serve immediately.

Nut Patties with Mango Relish

These spicy vegetarian patties can be made in advance, if you like, and reheated just before serving.

Serves 4–6

butter, for greasing
175g/6oz/1½ cups roasted
   and salted cashew nuts,
   finely chopped
175g/6oz/1½ cups walnuts,
   finely chopped
1 small onion, finely chopped
1 garlic clove, crushed
1 green chilli, seeded
   and chopped
5ml/1 tsp ground cumin
10ml/2 tsp ground coriander
2 carrots, coarsely grated
50g/2oz/1 cup fresh white
   breadcrumbs
30ml/2 tbsp chopped fresh
   coriander (cilantro)
15ml/1 tbsp lemon juice
1–2 eggs, lightly beaten
salt and ground black pepper
fresh coriander sprigs, to garnish

For the relish

1 large ripe mango, cut into
   small dice
1 small onion, cut into slivers
5ml/1 tsp grated fresh root ginger
pinch of salt
15ml/1 tbsp sesame oil
5ml/1 tsp black mustard seeds

1 Preheat the oven to 180°C/350°F/Gas 4. Lightly grease a baking sheet with butter.

2 Mix together the cashews, walnuts, onion, garlic, chilli, cumin, ground coriander, carrots, breadcrumbs and chopped coriander in a bowl and season with salt and pepper.

3 Sprinkle the lemon juice over the mixture and add enough of the beaten egg to bind it together. Using your hands, shape the mixture into twelve balls, then flatten slightly into round patties. Place them on the prepared baking sheet and bake for about 25 minutes, until golden brown.

4 To make the relish, mix together the mango, onion, fresh root ginger and salt. Heat the oil in a small frying pan, add the mustard seeds and cook for a few seconds until they pop and give off their aroma. Stir the seeds into the mango mixture and transfer the relish to a serving bowl. Serve with the nut patties, garnished with coriander sprigs.

Mussels Energy 289kcal/1211kJ; Protein 24g; Carbohydrate 10g, of which sugars 0.6g; Fat 15.2g, of which saturates 8.4g; Cholesterol 79mg; Calcium 333mg; Fibre 0.3g; Sodium 490mg.
Patties Energy 464kcal/1926kJ; Protein 12.8g; Carbohydrate 19.3g, of which sugars 8.4g; Fat 37.9g, of which saturates 5.2g; Cholesterol 32mg; Calcium 66mg; Fibre 3.5g; Sodium 167mg.

Dim Sum

A popular Chinese snack, these tiny dumplings are now fashionable in many specialist restaurants.

Serves 4
For the dough
150g/5oz/1¼ cups plain (all-purpose) flour
50ml/2fl oz/¼ cup boiling water
25ml/1½ tbsp cold water
7.5ml/1½ tsp vegetable oil

For the filling
75g/3oz minced (ground) pork

45ml/3 tbsp chopped canned bamboo shoots
7.5ml/½ tsp light soy sauce, plus extra to serve
5ml/1 tsp dry sherry
5ml/1 tsp demerara (raw) sugar
2.5ml/½ tsp sesame oil
5ml/1 tsp cornflour (cornstarch)

To serve
mixed fresh lettuce leaves such as iceberg, frisée or Webbs
spring onion (scallion) curls
sliced red chilli
prawn (shrimp) crackers

1 To make the dough, sift the flour into a bowl. Stir in the boiling water, then the cold water together with the oil. Mix to form a ball and knead until smooth. Divide the mixture into sixteen equal pieces and shape into rounds or half moon shapes.

2 For the filling, mix together the pork, bamboo shoots, soy sauce, sherry, sugar and oil. Then stir in the cornflour.

3 Place a little of the filling in the centre of each dim sum round. Carefully pinch the edges of the dough together to form little "purses".

4 Line a steamer with a damp dish towel. Place the dim sum in the steamer and steam for 5–10 minutes. Serve immediately on a bed of lettuce with soy sauce, spring onion curls, sweet chilli dipping sauce and prawn crackers if you like.

Variation
As an alternative filling, substitute cooked, peeled prawns (shrimp) for the pork.

Sesame Prawn Toasts

Serve about four of these delicious toasts per person with a soy sauce for dipping.

Serves 6
175g/6oz/1½ cups cooked, peeled prawns (shrimp)
2 spring onions (scallions), finely chopped
2.5cm/1in piece fresh root ginger, peeled and grated

2 garlic cloves, crushed
30ml/2 tbsp cornflour (cornstarch)
10ml/2 tsp soy sauce, plus extra for dipping
6 slices day-old bread from a small loaf, without crusts
40g/1½ oz sesame seeds
about 600ml/1 pint/2½ cups vegetable oil, for deep-frying

1 Place the prawns, spring onions, ginger and garlic cloves into a food processor fitted with a metal blade. Add the cornflour and soy sauce and process the mixture into a paste.

2 Spread the bread slices evenly with the paste and cut into triangles. Sprinkle with the sesame seeds, making sure they stick to the bread. Chill in the refrigerator for 30 minutes.

3 Heat the vegetable oil in a deep-fryer or large, heavy pan to 190°C/375°F or until a cube of day-old bread browns in 30 seconds. Using a slotted spoon, lower the toasts, in batches, into the oil, sesame-seed side down, and fry for 2–3 minutes, turning them over for the last minute. Remove with a slotted spoon and drain on absorbent kitchen paper. Keep the toasts warm while frying the remainder.

4 Place the toasts on individual dishes and serve immediately with little bowls of soy sauce for dipping.

Cook's Tip
Chinese soy sauce may be either light or dark. The former has a stronger flavour, while the latter is sweeter and is often used in cooking to give a richer colour to dishes. Light soy sauce is most usually used as a condiment and for dipping.

Dim Sum Energy 183kcal/773kJ; Protein 7.2g; Carbohydrate 31.5g, of which sugars 1.8g; Fat 3.8g, of which saturates 0.9g; Cholesterol 12mg; Calcium 55mg; Fibre 1.2g; Sodium 148mg.
Prawn Toasts Energy 207kcal/865kJ; Protein 8.7g; Carbohydrate 17.4g, of which sugars 1g; Fat 11.9g, of which saturates 1.5g; Cholesterol 57mg; Calcium 98mg; Fibre 1g; Sodium 427mg.

Sushi

Once barely known outside Japan, these tasty rolls of flavoured rice and paper-thin seaweed have become very popular.

Serves 4–6
To make the salmon sushi
2 eggs
10ml/2 tsp granulated sugar
2.5ml/½ tsp salt
10ml/2 tsp butter
3 sheets nori
150g/5oz fresh salmon fillet, cut into fingers

½ small cucumber, cut into strips
5ml/1 tsp thin wasabi paste

For the sushi rice
450g/1lb/4 cups sushi rice, rinsed
about 650ml/22fl oz/2¾ cups water
For the sushi dressing
60ml/4 tbsp rice vinegar
15ml/1 tbsp sugar
2.5ml/½ tsp salt
sliced pickled ginger, cut in strips, wasabi paste, thinned with water, Japanese sushi soy sauce, to serve

1 Place the rice in a heavy pan and add 650ml/22fl oz/2¾ cups water or according to the instructions on the packet. Meanwhile, blend together the rice vinegar, sugar and salt. Stir the dressing into the rice, then cover with a damp cloth and cool. Do not put in the fridge as this will make the rice go hard.

2 To make the salmon sushi, beat together the eggs with 30ml/2 tbsp water and the sugar and salt. Melt about one-third of the butter in a small frying pan and add one-third of the egg mixture to make an omelette. Repeat until you have three small omelettes.

3 Place a nori sheet, shiny side down, on a bamboo rolling mat, cover with an omelette and spread with sushi rice, leaving a 1cm/½in edge at the top and bottom. Lay strips of salmon across the width and lay cucumber strips next to the salmon. Spread a little wasabi paste over the salmon. Roll the nori around the filling. Wrap in clear film and chill for 10 minutes. Repeat to make three rolls. When the rolls are cool, remove the greaseproof paper and clear film. Using a wet knife, cut the rolls into six slices. Serve with pickled ginger, wasabi and Japanese sushi soy sauce.

Curried Eggs

Hard-boiled eggs are served on a mild creamy sauce with just a hint of curry.

Serves 2
4 eggs
15ml/1 tbsp sunflower oil
1 small onion, chopped
2.5cm/1in piece of fresh root ginger, grated
2.5ml/½ tsp ground cumin
2.5ml/½ tsp garam masala
22.5ml/1½ tbsp tomato purée (paste)
10ml/2 tsp tandoori paste
10ml/2 tsp freshly squeezed lemon juice
50ml/2fl oz/¼ cup single (light) cream
15ml/1 tbsp finely chopped fresh coriander (cilantro)
salt and ground black pepper
fresh coriander sprigs, to garnish

1 Put the eggs in a pan of water. Bring to the boil, lower the heat and simmer for 10 minutes.

2 Meanwhile, heat the oil in a frying pan over medium heat. Add the onion and cook, stirring occasionally, for 2–3 minutes. Add the ginger and cook, stirring constantly, for 1 minute more.

3 Stir in the ground cumin, garam masala, tomato purée, tandoori paste, lemon juice and cream. Cook for 1–2 minutes more, but do not allow the mixture to boil. Stir in the chopped coriander and season to taste with salt and pepper.

4 Drain the eggs, remove the shells and cut each egg in half. Spoon the sauce into a serving bowl, top with the eggs and garnish with fresh coriander. Serve immediately.

Cook's Tip
It is recommended that you store eggs in the refrigerator for health reasons. Do not wash them, but equally do not use dirty eggs. Store eggs pointed ends downwards, and remove from the refrigerator about 30 minutes before you want to cook them to allow them to come to room temperature. This will help prevent them from cracking.

Salmon Sushi Energy 191kcal/797kJ; Protein 8.2g; Carbohydrate 21.3g, of which sugars 7.7g; Fat 8.2g, of which saturates 1.4g; Cholesterol 19mg; Calcium 26mg; Fibre 0.9g; Sodium 442mg.
Curried Eggs Energy 310kcal/1286kJ; Protein 14.6g; Carbohydrate 2.7g, of which sugars 2.6g; Fat 27.2g, of which saturates 7.5g; Cholesterol 394mg; Calcium 133mg; Fibre 1.6g; Sodium 180mg.

Potatoes with Blue Cheese

So often served as a mere
accompaniment, potatoes
also make a satisfying main
dish, as here.

Serves 4
450g/1lb small new potatoes
small head of celery, sliced
small red onion, thinly sliced

115g/4oz blue cheese, mashed
150ml/¼ pint/⅔ cup single
 (light) cream
90g/3½ oz/scant 1 cup walnut
 pieces
30ml/2 tbsp chopped
 fresh parsley
salt and ground black pepper

1 Put the potatoes in a pan, add water to cover and bring to
the boil. Cook for about 15 minutes, adding the sliced celery
and onion to the pan for the last 5 minutes or so.

2 Drain the vegetables well and put them into a warmed,
shallow serving dish, making sure that they are evenly
distributed. Keep warm.

3 Put the cheese and cream in a small pan and melt over low
heat, stirring frequently. Do not allow the mixture to boil, but
heat it until it scalds.

4 Season the sauce to taste with salt and pepper, bearing in
mind that the cheese will already be quite salty. Pour it over the
vegetables and sprinkle the walnuts and chopped parsley over
the top. Serve immediately.

Cook's Tip
*Choose any blue cheese you like, such as Stilton, Danish blue,
Blue Vinney or blue Brie.*

Variation
*Substitute a thinly sliced fennel bulb for the celery if you like its
distinctive aniseed-like flavour.*

Greek Spinach & Cheese Pies

These individual spinach, feta
and Parmesan cheese pies
are easy to make using
ready-made filo pastry.

Makes 4
15ml/1 tbsp olive oil
1 small onion, finely chopped
275g/10oz/2½ cups spinach,
 stalks removed

50g/2oz/4 tbsp butter, melted
4 sheets filo pastry
1 egg
large pinch of freshly
 grated nutmeg
75g/3oz/¾ cup crumbled
 feta cheese
15ml/1 tbsp freshly grated
 Parmesan cheese
salt and ground black pepper

1 Preheat the oven to 190°C/375°F/Gas 5. Heat the oil in a
large pan over low heat. Add the onion and cook, stirring
occasionally, for 5–6 minutes, until softened. Add the spinach
leaves and cook, stirring, until the spinach has wilted and most
of the liquid has evaporated. Remove from the heat and leave
to cool completely.

2 Brush four 10cm/4in diameter loose-based tartlet tins (muffin
pans) with melted butter. Cut two sheets of filo into eight
14cm/4½in squares each.

3 Brush four squares at a time with melted butter. Line the first
tartlet tin with one square, gently easing it into the base and up
the sides. Leave the edges overhanging. Lay the remaining
squares on top of the first, turning them so the corners form a
star shape. Repeat for the remaining tins.

4 Beat the egg with the nutmeg and seasoning, then stir in the
cheeses and spinach. Divide the mixture among the tins and
smooth level. Fold the overhanging pastry over the filling.

5 Cut the third pastry sheet into eight 10cm/4in rounds. Brush
with butter and place two on top of each tartlet. Press around
the edges to seal. Brush the last pastry sheet with butter and
cut into strips. Gently twist each strip and lay them on top of
the tartlets. Bake for 30–35 minutes, until golden brown. Serve
the pies hot or cold.

Potatoes Energy 419kcal/1744kJ; Protein 13.3g; Carbohydrate 22g, of which sugars 4.8g; Fat 31.6g, of which saturates 11.4g; Cholesterol 42mg; Calcium 261mg; Fibre 3.6g; Sodium 439mg.
Cheese Pies Energy 287kcal/1191kJ; Protein 9.9g; Carbohydrate 17.2g, of which sugars 2.5g; Fat 20.3g, of which saturates 10.7g; Cholesterol 91mg; Calcium 269mg; Fibre 2.2g; Sodium 502mg.

Bombay Spiced Potatoes

A delicately aromatic mixture of whole and ground spices are used to flavour the potatoes in this classic Indian dish.

Serves 4
4 large potatoes (Maris Piper or King Edward), diced
60ml/4 tbsp sunflower oil
1 garlic clove, finely chopped

10ml/2 tsp brown mustard seeds
5ml/1 tsp black onion seeds (optional)
5ml/1 tsp ground turmeric
5ml/1 tsp ground cumin
5ml/1 tsp ground coriander
5ml/1 tsp fennel seeds
generous squeeze of lemon juice
salt and ground black pepper
chopped fresh coriander (cilantro) and lemon wedges, to garnish

1 Bring a pan of salted water to the boil, add the potatoes and simmer for about 4 minutes until just tender. Drain well.

2 Heat the oil in a large frying pan and add the garlic along with all the whole and ground spices. Stir-fry gently for 1–2 minutes until the mustard seeds start to pop.

3 Add the potatoes and stir-fry over medium heat for about 5 minutes, or until they are heated through and well coated with the spicy oil.

4 Season well with salt and pepper, then sprinkle over the lemon juice. Garnish with coriander and lemon wedges.

> **Cook's Tip**
> Keep an eye open for black onion seeds – kalonji – in Indian or Pakistani food stores.

> **Variation**
> For spiced potatoes and spinach, blanch about 450g/1lb fresh young spinach in boiling water for 2 minutes, then drain and squeeze dry. Add with the potatoes in step 3.

Spanish Chilli Potatoes

The Spanish name for this dish, *patatas bravas*, means fierce, hot potatoes. Reduce the amount of chilli if you find it too fiery.

Serves 4
900g/2lb new or salad potatoes
60ml/4 tbsp olive oil
1 onion, finely chopped
2 garlic cloves, crushed

15ml/1 tbsp tomato purée (paste)
200g/7oz can chopped tomatoes
15ml/1 tbsp red wine vinegar
2–3 small dried red chillies, seeded and chopped finely, or 5–10ml/1–2 tsp hot chilli powder
5ml/1 tsp paprika
salt and ground black pepper
fresh flat leaf parsley sprig, to garnish

1 Cook the potatoes in their skins in boiling water for 10–12 minutes, or until just tender. Drain them well and leave to cool, then cut in half and set aside.

2 Heat the oil in a large pan and fry the onion and garlic for 5–6 minutes until just softened. Stir in the tomato purée, tomatoes, vinegar, chilli and paprika and simmer for about 5 minutes.

3 Add the potatoes and mix into the sauce mixture to coat. Cover with a tight-fitting lid and simmer gently for about 8–10 minutes, or until the potatoes are tender.

4 Season well with salt and pepper, then transfer to a warmed serving dish. Serve, garnished with a sprig of flat leaf parsley.

> **Cook's Tip**
> Dried chillies will last for years, but they lose their savour over time, so buy only small quantities as you need them.

> **Variation**
> Stir in a few spoonfuls of sour cream at the end of step 3.

Bombay Spiced Energy 260kcal/1091kJ; Protein 4.8g; Carbohydrate 35.2g, of which sugars 2.8g; Fat 12.1g, of which saturates 1.5g; Cholesterol 0mg; Calcium 39mg; Fibre 3.4g; Sodium 40mg.
Spanish Chilli Energy 273kcal/1148kJ; Protein 4.6g; Carbohydrate 39.5g, of which sugars 5.9g; Fat 11.9g, of which saturates 1.9g; Cholesterol 0mg; Calcium 22mg; Fibre 3.1g; Sodium 39mg.

Florets Polonaise

Steamed vegetables make a delicious and extremely healthy accompaniment.

Serves 6

500g/1¼lb cauliflower and broccoli

finely grated rind of ½ lemon
1 large garlic clove, crushed
25g/1oz/½ cup wholegrain breadcrumbs, lightly baked or grilled (broiled) until crisp
2 eggs, hard-boiled and shelled
salt and ground black pepper

1 Trim the cauliflower and broccoli and break into florets, then place in a steamer over a pan of boiling water and steam for about 12 minutes. (If you prefer, boil the vegetables in salted water for 5–7 minutes, until just tender.) Drain the vegetables well and transfer to a warmed serving dish.

2 Meanwhile, make the topping. In a bowl, combine the lemon rind with the garlic and breadcrumbs. Finely chop the eggs and stir into the breadcrumb mixture. Season with salt and black pepper to taste, then sprinkle over the cooked vegetables.

Two Beans Provençal

This would make a tasty side dish for any main course.

Serves 4

5ml/1 tsp olive oil
1 small onion, finely chopped
1 garlic clove, crushed

225g/8oz/scant 1 cup green beans
225g/8oz/scant 1 cup runner (green) beans
2 tomatoes, peeled and chopped
salt and ground black pepper

1 Heat the oil in a heavy or non-stick frying pan, add the onion and sauté over medium heat until softened but not browned.

2 Add the garlic, both beans and the tomatoes. Season well with salt and pepper, then cover tightly. Cook over fairly low heat, shaking the pan from time to time, for about 30 minutes, or until the beans are tender. Serve immediately.

Spicy Jacket Potatoes

These lightly spiced potatoes make a glorious snack, light lunch or accompaniment to a meal.

Serves 2–4

2 large baking potatoes
5ml/1 tsp sunflower oil
1 small onion, chopped

2.5cm/1in piece fresh root ginger, grated
5ml/1 tsp ground cumin
5ml/1 tsp ground coriander
2.5ml/½ tsp ground turmeric
generous pinch of garlic salt
natural (plain) yogurt and fresh coriander (cilantro) sprigs, to serve

1 Preheat the oven to 220°C/425°F/Gas 7. Scrub the potatoes, then prick them all over with a fork. Bake for 1–1½ hours until tender. Remove them from the oven and reduce the temperature to 180°C/350°F/Gas 4.

2 Cut each potato in half and scoop out the flesh into a bowl. Place the potato shells on a baking sheet and return them to the oven to crisp up while you are making the filling.

3 Heat the oil in a non-stick frying pan, add the onion and fry for a few minutes until softened. Stir in the ginger, cumin, coriander and turmeric.

4 Stir over gentle heat for about 2 minutes, then add the potato flesh and garlic salt to taste. Mix well. Continue to cook the potato mixture gently for a further 2 minutes, stirring occasionally.

5 Remove the potato shells from the oven. Carefully spoon the potato mixture back into the shells and top each with a spoonful of natural yogurt and a sprig or two of fresh coriander. Serve immediately.

> **Cook's Tip**
> For the best results, choose a floury variety of potato, such as King Edward or Maris Piper.

Spicy Potatoes Energy 85kcal/361kJ; Protein 2g; Carbohydrate 17.6g, of which sugars 2.2g; Fat 1.2g, of which saturates 0.2g; Cholesterol 0mg; Calcium 18mg; Fibre 1.5g; Sodium 17mg.
Two Beans Energy 47kcal/195kJ; Protein 2.5g; Carbohydrate 6.3g, of which sugars 5.3g; Fat 1.4g, of which saturates 0.3g; Cholesterol 0mg; Calcium 46mg; Fibre 3.1g; Sodium 5mg.

Chinese Crispy Seaweed

In northern China, a special kind of seaweed is used for this dish, but spring greens make a very successful alternative. Serve as part of a Chinese spread.

Serves 4
225g/8oz spring greens (collards)
groundnut (peanut) or sunflower
    oil, for deep-frying
1.5ml/¼ tsp salt
10ml/2 tsp soft light brown sugar
30–45ml/2–3 tbsp toasted,
    flaked (sliced) almonds

1 Cut out and discard any tough stalks from the spring greens. Place about six leaves on top of each other, then roll them up into a tight roll.

2 Using a sharp knife, slice across into thin shreds. Lay on a tray and leave to dry for about 2 hours.

3 Heat about 5–7.5cm/2–3in of oil in a wok or pan to 190°C/375°F. Carefully place a handful of the leaves into the oil – it will bubble and spit for the first 10 seconds and then die down. Deep-fry for about 45 seconds, or until a slightly darker green: do not let the leaves burn.

4 Remove with a slotted spoon, drain on kitchen paper and transfer to a serving dish. Keep warm in the oven while frying the remainder.

5 When you have fried all the shredded leaves, sprinkle with the salt and sugar and toss lightly. Garnish with the toasted almonds and serve immediately.

Cook's Tips
• Make sure that your deep frying pan is deep enough to allow the oil to bubble up during cooking. The pan should be less than half full.
• The sugar gives the "seaweed" its characteristic sweet flavour; add to taste.

Leek & Parsnip Purée

This vegetable purée makes a delectable accompaniment to roasted meat or chicken.

Serves 4
2 large leeks, sliced
3 parsnips, sliced
knob (pat) of butter
45ml/3 tbsp top of the milk or
    single (light) cream
30ml/2 tbsp fromage frais or
    cream cheese
generous squeeze of lemon juice
salt and ground black pepper
large pinch of freshly grated
    nutmeg, to garnish

1 Steam or boil the leeks and parsnips together for about 15 minutes until tender. Drain well, then place in a food processor or blender.

2 Add the remaining ingredients and process until really smooth, then season with salt and pepper to taste. Transfer to a warmed bowl and garnish with a sprinkling of nutmeg.

Mexican-style Green Peas

This is a great way to make the most of fresh peas.

Serves 4
15ml/1 tbsp olive oil
2 garlic cloves, halved
1 onion, halved and thinly sliced
2 tomatoes, peeled, seeded and
    chopped into dice
400g/14oz/scant 3 cups shelled
    fresh peas
salt and ground black pepper
fresh chives, to garnish

1 Heat the oil in a pan and cook the garlic until golden. Scoop it out with a slotted spoon and discard. Add the onion to the pan and fry until translucent. Add the tomatoes and peas.

2 Pour 30ml/2 tbsp water into the pan and stir to mix. Lower the heat and cover the pan tightly. Cook for about 10 minutes, until the peas are cooked. Season with plenty of salt and pepper, then transfer the mixture to a heated dish. Garnish with fresh chives and serve immediately.

Crispy Seaweed Energy 171kcal/707kJ; Protein 3.3g; Carbohydrate 4.4g, of which sugars 3.9g; Fat 15.7g, of which saturates 1.7g; Cholesterol 0mg; Calcium 137mg; Fibre 2.5g; Sodium 13mg.
Leek Purée Energy 98kcal/413kJ; Protein 3.9g; Carbohydrate 13.3g, of which sugars 7.5g; Fat 3.6g, of which saturates 1.7g; Cholesterol 6mg; Calcium 75mg; Fibre 5.7g; Sodium 32mg.
Mexican Peas Energy 130kcal/541kJ; Protein 7.8g; Carbohydrate 15.6g, of which sugars 6.3g; Fat 4.6g, of which saturates 0.8g; Cholesterol 0mg; Calcium 32mg; Fibre 5.9g; Sodium 11mg.

Middle-Eastern Vegetable Stew

This spiced dish of mixed vegetables can be served as a side dish or as a vegetarian main course.

Serves 4–6

45ml/3 tbsp vegetable or chicken
  stock
1 green (bell) pepper, seeded and
  sliced
2 courgettes (zucchini), sliced
2 carrots, sliced
2 celery sticks, sliced
2 potatoes, diced
400g/14oz can chopped
  tomatoes
5ml/1 tsp chilli powder
30ml/2 tbsp chopped fresh mint
15ml/1 tbsp ground cumin
400g/14oz can chickpeas,
  drained
salt and ground black pepper
fresh mint sprigs, to garnish

1 Heat the vegetable or chicken stock in a large flameproof casserole until boiling, then add the sliced pepper, courgettes, carrots and celery. Stir over high heat for 2–3 minutes, until the vegetables are just beginning to soften.

2 Add the potatoes, tomatoes, chilli powder, mint and cumin. Add the chickpeas and bring to the boil.

3 Reduce the heat, cover the casserole with a tight-fitting lid and simmer for 30 minutes, or until all the vegetables are tender. Season to taste with salt and pepper and serve hot, garnished with mint leaves.

Cook's Tip
As a vegetarian main course, this dish is delicious with a couscous accompaniment. Soak 275g/10oz/1⅔ cups couscous in boiling vegetable stock for 10 minutes. Fluff up with a fork, then add about 15 pitted black olives, 2 small courgettes (zucchini) cut into strips and some toasted flaked (sliced) almonds. Whisk together 60ml/4 tbsp olive oil, 15ml/1 tbsp lemon juice and 15ml/1 tbsp each chopped coriander (cilantro) and parsley. Whisk in a pinch of cumin, cayenne pepper and salt. Pour the dressing over the salad and toss to mix.

Summer Vegetable Braise

Tender young vegetables are ideal for quick cooking in a minimum of liquid.

salt and ground black pepper
chopped fresh parsley and
  snipped fresh chives, to garnish

Serves 4

175g/6oz baby carrots
175g/6oz/1½ cups sugar snap
  peas or mangetouts
  (snow peas)
115g/4oz baby corn
90ml/6 tbsp vegetable stock
10ml/2 tsp lime juice

1 Place the baby carrots, peas and baby corn in a large heavy pan with the vegetable stock and lime juice. Bring to the boil.

2 Cover the pan and reduce the heat, then simmer for about 6–8 minutes, shaking the pan occasionally, until the vegetables are just tender.

3 Season the vegetables to taste with salt and pepper, then stir in the chopped fresh parsley and snipped fresh chives. Cook the vegetables for a few seconds more, stirring them once or twice until the herbs are well mixed, then serve.

Cook's Tip
This dish would be excellent for anyone on a low-fat diet.

Variations
• Mix and match the summer vegetables as you wish: asparagus and young broad beans would make good additions.
• You can cook a winter version of this dish using seasonal root vegetables. Cut the peeled vegetables into even-size chunks and cook for slightly longer.

Vegetable Stew Energy 149kcal/630kJ; Protein 7.8g; Carbohydrate 24.9g, of which sugars 6.8g; Fat 2.7g, of which saturates 0.4g; Cholesterol 0mg; Calcium 66mg; Fibre 5.7g; Sodium 172mg.
Summer Braise Energy 36kcal/151kJ; Protein 2.7g; Carbohydrate 5.9g, of which sugars 5.1g; Fat 0.3g, of which saturates 0.1g; Cholesterol 0mg; Calcium 33mg; Fibre 2.5g; Sodium 340mg.

Sweet Potatoes with Bacon

This sweet potato dish is often served for Thanksgiving in North America to celebrate the settlers' first harvest.

Serves 4

2 large sweet potatoes (about 450g/1lb each), washed
50g/2oz/½ cup soft light brown sugar
30ml/2 tbsp lemon juice
40g/1½ oz/3 tbsp butter, plus extra for greasing
4 rashers (strips) smoked streaky (fatty) bacon, cut into thin strips
salt and ground black pepper
sprig of flat leaf parsley, to garnish

1 Preheat the oven to 190°C/375°F/Gas 5 and lightly butter a shallow ovenproof dish. Cut the unpeeled sweet potatoes crossways into four and place the pieces in a pan of boiling water. Cover with a tight-fitting lid and cook for about 25 minutes until just tender.

2 Drain the potatoes and, when cool enough to handle, peel and slice quite thickly. Place in a single layer in the prepared dish, arranging so that each slice overlaps one another.

3 Sprinkle over the sugar and lemon juice and dot with butter. Top with the bacon and season with salt and pepper.

4 Bake, uncovered, for 35–40 minutes, basting once or twice, until the potatoes are tender.

5 Preheat the grill (broiler) to high. Grill (broil) the potatoes for about 2–3 minutes, until they are browned and the bacon crispy. Garnish with parsley and serve immediately.

> **Cook's Tip**
> *Sweet potatoes are now widely available in supermarkets. The orange-fleshed variety not only looks attractive but tastes delicious, particularly when the sweetness is enhanced, as here.*

Tex-Mex Baked Potatoes with Chilli

A great way to spice up baked potatoes – top them with a chilli bean sauce then serve with sour cream.

Serves 4

2 large potatoes
15ml/1 tbsp oil, plus extra for rubbing
1 garlic clove, crushed
1 small onion, chopped
½ small red (bell) pepper, seeded and chopped
225g/8oz/1 cup lean minced (ground) beef
½ small fresh red chilli, seeded and chopped
5ml/1 tsp ground cumin
pinch of cayenne pepper
200g/7oz can chopped tomatoes
30ml/2 tbsp tomato purée (paste)
2.5ml/½ tsp dried oregano
2.5ml/½ tsp dried marjoram
200g/7oz can red kidney beans, drained and rinsed
15ml/1 tbsp chopped fresh coriander (cilantro)
60ml/4 tbsp sour cream
salt and ground black pepper
chopped fresh parsley, to garnish

1 Preheat the oven to 220°C/425°F/Gas 7. Rub the potatoes with a little oil and pierce with a skewer. Bake them on the top shelf for about 1 hour until cooked through.

2 Meanwhile, heat the oil in a pan and fry the garlic, onion and pepper gently for 4–5 minutes, until softened.

3 Add the beef and cook over medium heat, stirring, until browned all over. Stir in the chilli, cumin, cayenne pepper, tomatoes, tomato purée, oregano and marjoram, then add 60ml/4 tbsp water.

4 Cover the pan with a tight-fitting lid and simmer for about 25 minutes, stirring occasionally.

5 Remove the lid, stir in the kidney beans and cook for 5 minutes. Turn off the heat and stir in the chopped fresh coriander. Season to taste with salt and pepper and set aside.

6 Cut the baked potatoes in half and place them in serving bowls. Top with the chilli mixture and a dollop of soured cream, then garnish with chopped fresh parsley. Serve immediately.

Sweet Potatoes Energy 291kcal/1220kJ; Protein 5.4g; Carbohydrate 37.1g, of which sugars 19.5g; Fat 14.5g, of which saturates 7.4g; Cholesterol 38mg; Calcium 37mg; Fibre 2.7g; Sodium 421mg.
Tex-Mex Energy 327kcal/1369kJ; Protein 17.7g; Carbohydrate 30.6g, of which sugars 8.2g; Fat 15.7g, of which saturates 6.4g; Cholesterol 43mg; Calcium 71mg; Fibre 5.2g; Sodium 277mg.

Fresh Tuna Salad Niçoise

Fresh tuna transforms this classic colourful salad from the south of France into something really special.

Serves 4
4 tuna steaks, about 150g/5oz each
30ml/2 tbsp olive oil
225g/8oz fine French beans, trimmed
1 small cos lettuce or 2 Little Gem lettuces
4 new potatoes, boiled
4 ripe tomatoes, or 12 cherry tomatoes

2 red peppers, seeded and cut into thin strips
4 hard-boiled eggs, sliced
8 drained anchovy fillets in oil, halved lengthways
16 large black olives
salt and ground black pepper
12 fresh basil leaves, to garnish

For the dressing
15ml/1 tbsp red wine vinegar
90ml/6 tbsp olive oil
1 fat garlic clove, crushed

1 Brush the tuna on both sides with a little olive oil and season. Heat a ridged grill (broiler) pan or the grill until very hot, then grill (broil) the tuna steaks for 1–2 minutes on each side.

2 Cook the beans in a pan of lightly salted boiling water for 4–5 minutes or until crisp-tender. Drain, refresh under cold water and drain again.

3 Separate the lettuce leaves and wash and dry them. Arrange them on four individual serving plates. Slice the potatoes and tomatoes, if large (leave cherry tomatoes whole) and divide them among the plates. Arrange the fine French beans and red pepper strips over them.

4 Shell the hard-boiled eggs, then cut them into thick slices. Place two half eggs on each plate with an anchovy fillet draped over. Arrange four olives on to each plate.

5 To make the dressing, whisk together the vinegar, olive oil and garlic and season to taste. Drizzle over the salads, arrange the tuna steaks on top, sprinkle over the basil and serve.

Hot Tomato & Mozzarella Salad

A quick, easy appetizer with a Mediterranean flavour.

Serves 4
450g/1lb plum tomatoes, sliced
225g/8oz mozzarella cheese
1 red onion, chopped
4–6 pieces sun-dried tomatoes in oil, drained and chopped

60ml/4 tbsp olive oil
5ml/1 tsp red wine vinegar
2.5ml/½ tsp Dijon mustard
60ml/4 tbsp mixed chopped fresh herbs such as basil, parsley, oregano and chives
salt and ground black pepper
fresh herb sprigs, to garnish (optional)

1 Arrange the sliced tomatoes and mozzarella in circles in four shallow flameproof dishes. Sprinkle with the onion and sun-dried tomatoes. Whisk together the olive oil, vinegar, mustard, chopped herbs and seasoning. Pour over the salads.

2 Place the salads under a hot grill (broiler)for 4–5 minutes, until the mozzarella starts to melt. Grind over plenty of black pepper and serve garnished with fresh herb sprigs, if you like.

Devilled Kidneys

This tangy dish makes an impressive appetizer.

Serves 4
10ml/2tsp Worcestershire sauce
15ml/1 tbsp English (hot) mustard
15ml/1 tbsp lemon juice

15ml/1 tbsp tomato purée (paste)
40g/1½oz/3 tbsp butter
1 shallot, chopped
8 prepared lamb's kidneys
salt and cayenne pepper
chopped fresh parsley, to garnish

1 Mix together the Worcestershire sauce, mustard, lemon juice and tomato purée in a bowl. Season with cayenne and salt.

2 Melt the butter in a frying pan and cook the shallot for 5 minutes. Stir in the kidneys and cook for 3 minutes on each side. Coat with the sauce and serve, sprinkled with parsley.

Salad Energy 301kcal/1250kJ; Protein 11.8g; Carbohydrate 6.2g, of which sugars 5.9g; Fat 25.7g, of which saturates 9.9g; Cholesterol 33mg; Calcium 219mg; Fibre 1.8g; Sodium 237mg.
Kidneys Energy 140kcal/584kJ; Protein 10.8g; Carbohydrate 2.3g, of which sugars 1.9g; Fat 9.9g, of which saturates 5.7g; Cholesterol 210mg; Calcium 24mg; Fibre 24g; Sodium 191mg.
Niçoise Energy 578kcal/2408kJ; Protein 46.4g; Carbohydrate 15g, of which sugars 10.6g; Fat 37.5g, of which saturates 7.1g; Cholesterol 235mg; Calcium 127mg; Fibre 4.7g; Sodium 585mg.

Mexican Dip with Chips

This appetizer also makes a fabulous snack to serve with pre-dinner drinks.

Serves 4
2 avocados
juice of 1 lime
½ small onion, finely chopped
½ red chilli, seeded and
  finely chopped
3 tomatoes, peeled, seeded and
  finely diced
30ml/2 tbsp chopped fresh
  coriander (cilantro)

30ml/2 tbsp sour cream
salt and ground black pepper
15 ml/1 tbsp sour cream and
  a pinch of cayenne pepper,
  to garnish

For the chips
150g/5oz bag tortilla chips
30ml/2 tbsp finely grated mature
  (sharp) Cheddar cheese
1.5ml/¼ tsp chilli powder
10ml/2 tsp chopped fresh parsley

1 Halve and stone (pit) the avocados and scoop the flesh with a spoon, scraping the shells well. Place the flesh in a blender or food processor with the remaining dip ingredients, reserving the sour cream and cayenne pepper for the garnish. Process until fairly smooth. Transfer to a bowl, cover with clear film (plastic wrap) and chill in the refrigerator until required.

2 To make the chips, preheat the grill (broiler), then spread out the tortilla chips on a baking sheet. Mix the grated cheese with the chilli powder, sprinkle over the chips and grill (broil) for 1–2 minutes, until the cheese has melted.

3 Remove the avocado dip from the refrigerator, top with the sour cream and sprinkle with cayenne pepper. Serve the bowl on a plate surrounded by the tortilla chips, garnished with the chopped fresh parsley.

> **Cook's Tip**
> You can omit the fresh chilli and the chilli powder if you prefer the dip to have a milder flavour or you are planning to serve it to young children.

Potted Shrimp

Sometimes the simplest recipes are the best and this classic English appetizer has stood the test of time and remains very popular.

Serves 4
225g/8oz/2 cups shelled shrimp

225g/8oz/1 cup butter
pinch of ground mace
salt and cayenne pepper
fresh dill sprigs, to garnish
lemon wedges and thin slices
  of brown bread and butter,
  to serve

1 Chop a quarter of the shrimp. Melt half the butter over low heat, carefully skimming off any foam that rises to the surface.

2 Stir the chopped and whole shrimp and the mace into the pan, season to taste with salt and cayenne pepper and heat gently without boiling. Pour the shrimp and butter mixture into four individual pots or ramekins and set aside to cool.

3 Heat the remaining butter in a clean small pan, then carefully spoon the clear butter over the shrimp, leaving the sediment behind in the pan.

4 Leave until the butter is almost set, then place a dill sprig in the centre of each pot. Leave to set completely, then cover and chill in the refrigerator.

5 Remove the potted shrimps from the refrigerator about 30 minutes before serving to bring to room temperature. Serve with lemon wedges and thin slices of brown bread and butter.

> **Cook's Tip**
> This dish is traditionally prepared with the tiny European brown shrimp found off the east coast of England. They have a incomparably delicate flavour but are very boring to peel. You can substitute small prawns (US small to medium shrimp) if you like. In that case, chop between a third and half the shellfish in step 1.

Shrimp Energy 461kcal/1901kJ; Protein 10.3g; Carbohydrate 0.4g, of which sugars 0.4g; Fat 46.6g, of which saturates 29.4g; Cholesterol 230mg; Calcium 55mg; Fibre 0g; Sodium 448mg.
Dip Energy 332kcal/1385kJ; Protein 6.6g; Carbohydrate 27.3g, of which sugars 4.2g; Fat 22.3g, of which saturates 6.2g; Cholesterol 12mg; Calcium 133mg; Fibre 4.9g; Sodium 390mg.

French Goat's Cheese Salad

The deep, tangy flavours of this salad would also make it satisfying enough for a light meal, if you wished.

Serves 4

200g/7oz bag prepared mixed
   salad leaves including some soft
   and bitter varieties
4 rashers (strips) rindless lean
   back bacon
16 thin slices French bread
115g/4oz/½ cup full-fat
   goat's cheese

For the dressing
60ml/4 tbsp olive oil
15ml/1 tbsp tarragon vinegar
10ml/2 tsp walnut oil
5ml/1 tsp Dijon mustard
5ml/1 tsp wholegrain mustard
salt and ground black pepper

1 Preheat the grill (broiler). Rinse and dry the salad leaves, then arrange them in four individual serving bowls. Set aside in a cool place but not the refrigerator.

2 To make the dressing, pout the olive oil, vinegar, walnut oil and both types of mustard in a screw-top jar. Close the lid and shake well until combined. Season and set aside until required.

3 Lay the bacon rashers flat on a board, then stretch them using the back of a knife. Cut each rasher into four pieces. Roll up each piece up and secure with a wooden cocktail stick (toothpick). Grill (broil) for about 2–3 minutes, until golden on one side of the rolls.

4 Meanwhile, slice the goat's cheese into eight and halve each slice. Top each slice of bread with a piece of goat's cheese and place under the grill. Turn over the bacon rolls and continue cooking with the goat's cheese toasts until the cheese is golden and bubbling and the bacon rolls are cooked through.

5 Arrange the bacon rolls and toasts on top of the prepared salad leaves. Shake the dressing well again to mix and spoon a little of it over each serving. Serve immediately.

Russian Salad

This hearty salad became fashionable in the hotel dining rooms of Europe in the 1920s and 1930s.

Serves 4

115g/4oz large button (white)
   mushrooms
120ml/4fl oz/½ cup mayonnaise
15ml/1 tbsp lemon juice
350g/12oz peeled, cooked
   prawns (shrimp)
1 large dill pickle, finely chopped,
   or 30ml/2 tbsp capers

115g/4oz broad (fava) beans
115g/4oz small new potatoes,
   scrubbed or scraped
115g/4oz young carrots, trimmed
   and peeled
115g/4oz baby sweetcorn
115g/4oz baby turnips, trimmed
15ml/1 tbsp olive oil, preferably
   French or Italian
4 hard-boiled eggs, shelled
salt and ground black pepper
25g/1oz canned anchovy fillets,
   cut into fine strips, to garnish
paprika, to garnish

1 Slice the mushrooms thinly, then cut into matchsticks. Combine the mayonnaise and lemon juice. Fold the mayonnaise into the mushrooms and prawns, add the dill pickle or capers, then season to taste with salt and pepper.

2 Bring a large pan of salted water to the boil, add the broad beans and cook for 3 minutes. Drain and cool under running water, then pinch the beans between thumb and forefinger to release them from their tough skins.

3 Boil the potatoes for 20 minutes and the remaining vegetables for 6 minutes. Drain and cool under running water.

4 Toss the vegetables with the olive oil and divide among four shallow bowls. Spoon on the dressed prawns and place a hard-boiled egg in the centre. Garnish the egg with strips of anchovy and sprinkle with paprika. Serve immediately.

Cook's Tip
It's worth the effort of removing the broad bean skins, as the bright green beans beneath are exceptionally tender.

Goat's Cheese Energy 498kcal/2087kJ; Protein 19.6g; Carbohydrate 48.9g, of which sugars 3.5g; Fat 26.3g, of which saturates 8.8g; Cholesterol 40mg; Calcium 230mg; Fibre 3.2g; Sodium 1152mg.
Russian Salad Energy 455kcal/1890kJ; Protein 28.1g; Carbohydrate 12.8g, of which sugars 5g; Fat 32.8g, of which saturates 5.7g; Cholesterol 387mg; Calcium 162mg; Fibre 4.3g; Sodium 963mg.

Classic Greek Salad

Anyone who has spent a holiday in Greece will have eaten a version of this salad – the Greek equivalent to a mixed salad.

Serves 4
1 cos lettuce
½ cucumber, halved lengthways

4 tomatoes
8 spring onions (scallions)
75g/3oz Greek black olives
115g/4oz feta cheese
90ml/6 tbsp white wine vinegar
150ml/¼ pint/⅔ cup extra virgin olive oil
salt and ground black pepper
rustic bread, to serve (optional)

1 Tear the lettuce leaves into pieces and place them in a large serving bowl. Slice the cucumber and add to the bowl.

2 Cut the tomatoes into wedges and put them into the bowl.

3 Slice the spring onions. Add them to the bowl along with the olives and toss well.

4 Cut the feta cheese into dice and add to the salad.

5 Put the vinegar and olive oil into a small bowl and season to taste with salt and pepper. Whisk well. Pour the dressing over the salad and toss to combine. Serve at once with extra olives and chunks of bread, if you wish.

Cook's Tips
• *This salad can be assembled in advance, but should only be dressed just before serving. Keep the dressing at room temperature as chilling deadens its flavours.*
• *The success of this salad relies on using the freshest of ingredients and a good olive oil.*

Variation
The lettuce can be left out for a salad with a bit more bite.

Avocado, Tomato & Mozzarella

This popular, attractive salad is made from ingredients representing the colours of the Italian flag – a sunny, cheerful dish! The addition of pasta turns it into a main course for a light lunch.

Serves 4
175g/6oz/1½ cups farfalle
6 ripe red tomatoes
225g/8oz mozzarella cheese
1 large ripe avocado

30ml/2 tbsp chopped fresh basil
30ml/2 tbsp pine nuts, toasted
fresh basil sprig, to garnish

For the dressing
90ml/6 tbsp olive oil
30ml/2 tbsp wine vinegar
5ml/1 tsp balsamic vinegar (optional)
5ml/1 tsp wholegrain mustard
pinch of sugar
salt and ground black pepper

1 Bring a large pan of lightly salted water to the boil and cook the pasta bows until *al dente*.

2 Slice the tomatoes and mozzarella cheese into thin rounds. Halve the avocado, remove the stone (pit) and peel off the skin. Slice the flesh lengthways.

3 Place the dressing ingredients in a small bowl and whisk together to combine.

4 Arrange the tomato, mozzarella and avocado slices in overlapping slices around the edge of a flat serving plate.

5 Toss the pasta with half of the dressing and the chopped basil. Pile into the centre of the plate. Pour over the remaining dressing, scatter over the pine nuts and garnish with basil.

Cook's Tip
The pale green flesh of the avocado quickly discolours once it is cut. Prepare it at the last minute and place immediately in dressing. If you must prepare it ahead, squeeze lemon juice over the cut side and cover with clear film (plastic wrap).

Greek Salad Energy 347kcal/1433kJ; Protein 6.3g; Carbohydrate 5.4g, of which sugars 5.3g; Fat 33.5g, of which saturates 8g; Cholesterol 20mg; Calcium 148mg; Fibre 2.5g; Sodium 849mg.
Avocado Energy 612kcal/2552kJ; Protein 18.8g; Carbohydrate 38.3g, of which sugars 6.6g; Fat 43.7g, of which saturates 12.7g; Cholesterol 33mg; Calcium 231mg; Fibre 4.6g; Sodium 240mg.

Californian Salad

Full of vitality and vitamins, this is a lovely light and healthy salad for sunny summer days.

Serves 4

1 small crisp lettuce, torn into pieces
225g/8oz/4 cups young spinach leaves
2 carrots, coarsely grated
115g/4oz cherry tomatoes, halved
2 celery sticks, thinly sliced
75g/3oz/½ cup raisins
50g/2oz/½ cup blanched almonds or unsalted cashew nuts, halved
30ml/2 tbsp sunflower seeds
30ml/2 tbsp sesame seeds, lightly toasted

For the dressing

45ml/3 tbsp extra virgin olive oil
30ml/2 tbsp cider vinegar
10ml/2 tsp clear honey
juice of 1 small orange
salt and ground black pepper

1 Put the lettuce, spinach, carrots, tomatoes and celery in a large bowl. Add the raisins, almonds and the sunflower and sesame seeds.

2 Put all the dressing ingredients in a screw-top jar and shake well to combine, then pour over the salad.

3 Toss the salad thoroughly and divide among four small salad bowls. Season with salt and pepper and serve immediately.

Cook's Tips
• For tomato and mozzarella toasts to serve with the salad, cut French bread diagonally into slices, then toast lightly on both sides. Spread some sun-dried tomato paste on one side of each slice. Cut some mozzarella into small pieces and arrange over the tomato paste. Put on baking sheets, sprinkle with chopped herbs and black pepper to taste and drizzle with olive oil. Bake in a hot oven for 5 minutes or until the mozzarella has melted. Leave to settle for a few minutes before serving.
• If the tomatoes are hard and tasteless, try roasting them in the oven with a little olive oil, then add to the salad.

Scandinavian Cucumber & Dill

This refreshing salad is good with hot and spicy food.

Serves 4

2 cucumbers
30ml/2 tbsp snipped fresh chives
30ml/2 tbsp chopped fresh dill
150ml/¼ pint/⅔ cup sour cream or fromage frais
salt and ground black pepper

1 Slice the cucumbers as thinly as possible, preferably in a food processor or with a slicer. Place the slices in layers in a colander (strainer), sprinkling each layer evenly, but not too heavily, with salt. Set over a plate to catch the juices.

2 Leave the cucumber to drain for up to 2 hours, then lay out the slices on a clean dish towel and pat them dry. Mix the cucumber with the herbs, cream or fromage frais and plenty of pepper. Serve immediately.

Spinach & Roast Garlic Salad

This salad makes the most of the health-giving qualities of spinach and garlic.

Serves 4

12 garlic cloves, unpeeled
60ml/4 tbsp extra virgin olive oil
450g/1lb/8 cups baby spinach leaves
50g/2oz/½ cup pine nuts, lightly toasted
juice of ½ lemon
salt and ground black pepper

1 Preheat the oven to 190°C/375°F/Gas 5. Place the unpeeled garlic cloves in a small roasting pan, drizzle over 30ml/2 tbsp of the olive oil and toss to coat. Bake for about 15 minutes until slightly charred.

2 Place the garlic cloves, still in their skins, in a salad bowl. Add the spinach, pine nuts, lemon juice and remaining olive oil. Toss well and season with salt and pepper. Serve immediately, gently squeezing the softened garlic purée out of the skins to eat.

Californian Energy 319kcal/1327kJ; Protein 7.9g; Carbohydrate 23.5g, of which sugars 21.7g; Fat 22.1g, of which saturates 2.6g; Cholesterol 0mg; Calcium 205mg; Fibre 5g; Sodium 114mg.
Scandinavian Energy 88kcal/361kJ; Protein 1.9g; Carbohydrate 2.8g, of which sugars 2.7g; Fat 7.7g, of which saturates 4.7g; Cholesterol 23mg; Calcium 69mg; Fibre 1g; Sodium 21mg.
Spinach Energy 222kcal/915kJ; Protein 5.1g; Carbohydrate 4g, of which sugars 3.5g; Fat 20.7g, of which saturates 2.3g; Cholesterol 0mg; Calcium 238mg; Fibre 4.1g; Sodium 23mg.

Chinese Special Fried Rice

This staple of Chinese cuisine consists of a mixture of chicken, shrimps and vegetables with fried rice.

Serves 4

200g/7oz/1 cup long grain white rice
45ml/3 tbsp groundnut (peanut) oil
1 garlic clove, crushed
4 spring onions (scallions), finely chopped
115g/4oz/1 cup diced cooked chicken

115g/4oz/1 cup peeled, cooked shrimps
50g/2oz/½ cup frozen peas
1 egg, beaten with a pinch of salt
50g/2oz/1 cup finely shredded lettuce
30ml/2 tbsp light soy sauce
pinch of caster (superfine) sugar
salt and ground black pepper
15ml/1 tbsp chopped, roasted cashew nuts, to garnish

1 Rinse the rice in two to three changes of warm water to wash away some of the starch. Drain well.

2 Put the rice in a pan and add 15ml/1 tbsp of the oil and 350ml/12fl oz/1½ cups water. Cover and bring to the boil, stir once, then cover and simmer for 12–15 minutes, until nearly all the water has been absorbed. Turn off the heat, cover and leave to stand for 10 minutes. Fluff up with a fork and leave to cool.

3 Heat the remaining oil in a wok or frying pan and stir-fry the garlic and spring onions for 30 seconds.

4 Add the chicken, shrimps and peas and stir-fry for about 1–2 minutes, then add the cooked rice and stir-fry for a further 2 minutes. Pour in the egg and stir-fry until just set. Stir in the lettuce, soy sauce, sugar and salt and pepper to taste.

5 Transfer to a warmed serving bowl, sprinkle with the chopped cashew nuts and serve immediately.

> **Cook's Tip**
> When using a wok, preheat it before adding the oil. Swirl the oil around the sides and heat it up before adding the ingredients.

Lemony Bulgur Wheat Salad

This Middle-Eastern salad, called *tabbouleh*, is delicious as an accompaniment to grilled meats or fish, or on its own as a light snack.

Serves 4

2 tomatoes, peeled and chopped
225g/8oz/1½ cups bulgur wheat
4 spring onions (scallions), finely chopped

75ml/5 tbsp chopped fresh mint
75ml/5 tbsp chopped fresh parsley
15ml/1 tbsp chopped fresh coriander (cilantro)
juice of 1 lemon
75ml/5 tbsp olive oil
salt and ground black pepper
fresh mint sprigs, to garnish

1 Make a slash in the skin of each tomato, then put them all in a heatproof bowl and pour over boiling water. Leave for 30 seconds, then plunge the tomatoes into cold water. Peel and seed, then roughly chop the flesh. Set aside.

2 Place the bulgur wheat in a bowl, pour on enough boiling water to cover and leave to soak for 20 minutes.

3 Line a colander with a clean dish towel. Turn the soaked bulgur wheat into the centre, let it drain, then gather up the sides of the dish towel and squeeze out any remaining liquid. Turn the bulgur wheat into a large bowl.

4 Add the spring onions, mint, parsley, coriander and tomatoes. Mix well, then pour over the lemon juice and olive oil. Season generously with salt and pepper, then toss so that all the ingredients are combined.

5 Chill in the refrigerator for a couple of hours before serving, garnished with mint.

> **Variation**
> Add some pitted, halved black olives to the salad just before serving for extra tangy flavour.

Fried Rice Energy 343kcal/1434kJ; Protein 20.2g; Carbohydrate 40.5g, of which sugars 4.2g; Fat 11.2g, of which saturates 1.6g; Cholesterol 124mg; Calcium 91mg; Fibre 2.4g; Sodium 632mg.
Wheat Salad Energy 194kcal/811kJ; Protein 4.3g; Carbohydrate 31.2g, of which sugars 2.3g; Fat 6.5g, of which saturates 0.9g; Cholesterol 0mg; Calcium 56mg; Fibre 1.6g; Sodium 12mg.

Tanzanian Vegetable Rice

This light, fluffy dish of steamed rice flavoured with colourful vegetables makes a versatile accompaniment.

Serves 4–6
350g/12oz/2 cups basmati rice
45ml/3 tbsp vegetable oil

1 onion, chopped
750ml/1¼ pints/3 cups vegetable stock or water
2 garlic cloves, crushed
115g/4oz/1 cup sweetcorn
½ fresh red or green (bell) pepper, chopped
1 large carrot, grated

1 Rinse the rice in a sieve (strainer) under cold water, then leave to drain for about 15 minutes.

2 Heat the oil in a large pan, add the onion and fry for a few minutes over medium heat until just softened.

3 Add the rice and stir-fry for about 10 minutes, taking care to stir continuously so that the rice does not stick to the bottom of the pan.

4 Add the stock or water and the garlic and stir well. Bring to the boil and cook over high heat for 5 minutes, then reduce the heat, cover with a tight-fitting lid and leave the rice to cook for 20 minutes.

5 Scatter the corn over the rice, then spread the pepper on top and lastly sprinkle over the grated carrot.

6 Cover tightly and continue to steam over low heat until the rice is cooked. Gently fork through the rice to fluff up and serve immediately.

> **Variation**
> Vary the vegetables according to what you have to hand. Sliced courgettes (zucchini) or small broccoli florets would work well, while frozen peas make an easy, colourful addition. Defrost them before adding to the rice.

Indian Pilau Rice

Basmati rice is simply flavoured with aromatic spices and seeds to create a delightfully fragrant dish.

Serves 4
225g/8oz/1¼ cups basmati rice, rinsed well
30ml/2 tbsp vegetable oil
1 small onion, finely chopped
1 garlic clove, crushed
5ml/1 tsp fennel seeds
15ml/1 tbsp sesame seeds

2.5ml/½ tsp ground turmeric
5ml/1 tsp ground cumin
1.5ml/¼ tsp salt
2 whole cloves
4 green cardamom pods, lightly crushed
5 black peppercorns
450ml/¾ pint/scant 2 cups chicken stock
15ml/1 tbsp ground almonds
fresh coriander (cilantro) sprigs, to garnish

1 Soak the rice in water for 30 minutes. Heat the oil in a pan, and fry the onions and garlic gently for 5–6 minutes, until soft.

2 Stir in the fennel and sesame seeds, the turmeric, cumin, salt, cloves, cardamom pods and peppercorns and cook for about 1 minute. Drain the rice well, add to the pan and stir-fry for a further 3 minutes.

3 Pour on the chicken stock. Bring to the boil, then cover with a tight-fitting lid, reduce the heat to very low and simmer gently for 20 minutes, without removing the lid, until all the liquid has been absorbed.

4 Remove from the heat and leave to stand for 2–3 minutes. Fluff up the rice with a fork and stir in the ground almonds. Garnish with coriander sprigs and serve immediately.

> **Cook's Tips**
> • Basmati rice is the most popular choice for Indian dishes, but you could use long grain rice instead.
> • Green cardamoms are more suitable for this dish than the black variety as they are more delicate in flavour and texture.

Tanzanian Energy 449kcal/1877kJ; Protein 8.1g; Carbohydrate 83g, of which sugars 7.7g; Fat 9.3g, of which saturates 1.1g; Cholesterol 0mg; Calcium 30mg; Fibre 1.8g; Sodium 85mg.
Pilau Rice Energy 302kcal/1258kJ; Protein 5.8g; Carbohydrate 46.4g, of which sugars 1g; Fat 10.1g, of which saturates 1.1g; Cholesterol 0mg; Calcium 49mg; Fibre 0.8g; Sodium 2mg.

Sole Goujons with Lime Mayonnaise

This simple French dish can be rustled up very quickly. It makes an excellent light lunch or supper.

Serves 4
675g/1½lb sole fillets, skinned
2 eggs, beaten
115g/4oz/2 cups fresh
   white breadcrumbs
vegetable oil, for deep-frying
salt and ground black pepper
lime wedges, to serve

For the lime mayonnaise
200ml/7fl oz/scant 1 cup
   mayonnaise
1 small garlic clove, crushed
10ml/2 tsp capers, rinsed
   and chopped
10ml/2 tsp chopped gherkins
finely grated rind of ½ lime
10ml/2 tsp lime juice
15ml/1 tbsp chopped fresh
   coriander (cilantro)

1 To make the lime mayonnaise, mix together the mayonnaise, garlic, capers, gherkins, lime rind and juice and chopped coriander in a bowl. Season to taste with salt and pepper. Transfer to a serving bowl, cover with clear film (plastic wrap) and chill in the refrigerator until required.

2 Cut the sole fillets into finger-length strips. Dip them first into the beaten eggs and then into the breadcrumbs.

3 Heat the oil in a deep-fat fryer or large, heavy pan to 180°C/350°F, or until a cube of day-old bread browns in 30 seconds. Add the fish, in batches, and cook until golden and crisp. Remove from the oil and drain well on kitchen paper.

4 Pile the goujons on to warmed serving plates and serve with the lime wedges for squeezing over. Serve the lime mayonnaise separately.

Cook's Tip
Make sure you use good quality mayonnaise for the sauce, or – better still – make your own. But remember that pregnant women, the elderly and the very young should not eat raw egg.

Spicy Fish Rösti

Serve these delicious Swiss-style patties crisp and hot for lunch or supper with a mixed green salad.

Serves 4
350g/12oz large, firm
   waxy potatoes
350g/12oz salmon fillet, skinned
3–4 spring onions (scallions),
   finely chopped

5ml/1 tsp grated fresh root ginger
30ml/2 tbsp chopped fresh
   coriander (cilantro)
10ml/2 tsp lemon juice
30–45ml/2–3 tbsp sunflower oil
salt and cayenne pepper
lemon wedges, to serve
fresh coriander sprigs, to garnish

1 Bring a pan of water to the boil, add the potatoes with their skins on and cook for about 10 minutes. Drain and leave to cool for a few minutes.

2 Meanwhile, finely chop the salmon and place in a bowl. Stir in the spring onions, ginger, chopped coriander and lemon juice. Season to taste with salt and cayenne pepper.

3 When the potatoes are cool enough to handle, peel off the skins and grate the flesh coarsely. Gently stir the grated potato into the fish mixture. Form the mixture into 12 patties, pressing the mixture together but leaving the edges slightly uneven.

4 Heat the oil in a large frying pan over medium heat. Add the fish rösti, a few at a time, and cook for 3 minutes on each side, until golden brown and crisp. Remove from the pan and drain on kitchen paper. Keep warm while you cook the remaining rösti. Serve hot with lemon wedges for squeezing over and garnished with sprigs of fresh coriander.

Variation
You can also make these tasty patties with cod or coley (pollock) fillet or with a mixture of 225g/8oz white fish fillet and 115g/4 oz salmon fillet.

Sole Energy 978kcal/4047kJ; Protein 26.8g; Carbohydrate 25.2g, of which sugars 2.4g; Fat 86.3g, of which saturates 11.1g; Cholesterol 127mg; Calcium 87mg; Fibre 0.1g; Sodium 546mg.
Rösti Energy 208kcal/870kJ; Protein 17.7g; Carbohydrate 14.4g, of which sugars 1.4g; Fat 9.2g, of which saturates 1.2g; Cholesterol 40mg; Calcium 17mg; Fibre 1g; Sodium 63mg.

Mediterranean Fish Rolls

Sun-dried tomatoes, pine nuts and anchovies make a flavoursome stuffing for the fish.

Serves 4

75g/3oz/6 tbsp butter, plus extra for greasing
4 plaice or flounder fillets (about 225g/8oz each), skinned
1 small onion, chopped
1 celery stick, finely chopped

115g/4oz/2 cups fresh white breadcrumbs
45ml/3 tbsp chopped fresh parsley
30ml/2 tbsp pine nuts, toasted
3–4 pieces sun-dried tomatoes in oil, drained and chopped
50g/2oz can anchovy fillets, drained and chopped
75ml/5 tbsp fish stock
ground black pepper

1 Preheat the oven to 180°C/350°F/Gas 4. Grease a shallow, ovenproof dish with butter. Using a sharp knife, cut the fish fillets in half lengthways to make eight smaller fillets.

2 Melt the butter in a heavy pan over low heat. Add the onion and celery, cover with a tight-fitting lid and cook, stirring occasionally, for about 15 minutes, until the vegetables are very soft but not coloured.

3 Mix together the breadcrumbs, parsley, pine nuts, sun-dried tomatoes and anchovies in a bowl. Stir in the softened vegetables with the buttery pan juices and season to taste with pepper.

4 Divide the stuffing into eight equal portions. Taking one portion at a time, form the stuffing into balls, then roll up each one inside a fish fillet. Secure each roll with a wooden cocktail stick (toothpick).

5 Place the rolled-up fillets in the prepared dish. Pour the fish stock over them and cover the dish with buttered foil. Bake for about 20 minutes, or until the fish flakes easily with the point of a sharp knife. Remove and discard the cocktail sticks, transfer the fish rolls to warmed plates, drizzle a little of the cooking juices over them and serve immediately.

Salmon with Watercress Sauce

Adding the watercress right at the end of cooking retains much of its flavour and colour.

Serves 4

300ml/1/2 pint/1 1/4 cups crème fraîche
30ml/2 tbsp chopped fresh tarragon
25g/1oz/2 tbsp butter

15ml/1 tbsp sunflower oil
4 salmon fillets, skinned
1 garlic clove, crushed
120ml/4fl oz/1/2 cup dry white wine
1 bunch of watercress or rocket (arugula)
salt and ground black pepper
mixed lettuce salad, to serve (optional)

1 Gently heat the crème fraîche in a small pan until it is just beginning to boil. Remove the pan from the heat and stir in half the tarragon. Leave the herb cream to infuse (steep) while cooking the fish.

2 Heat the butter and oil in a heavy frying pan over medium heat. Add the salmon fillets and cook for 3–5 minutes on each side. Remove them from the pan and keep warm.

3 Add the garlic to the pan and cook for 1 minute, then pour in the wine and leave it to bubble until it has reduced to about 15ml/1 tbsp.

4 Meanwhile, strip the leaves off the watercress stalks and chop them finely. Discard any damaged leaves. (Save the watercress stalks for soup, if you like.) If using rocket, trim the stems and chop the leaves finely.

5 Strain the herb cream into the frying pan and cook, stirring constantly, for a few minutes, until the sauce has thickened. Stir in the remaining tarragon and watercress or rocket, then cook for a few minutes, until the leaves have wilted but are still bright green. Season to taste with salt and pepper. Place the salmon fillets on warmed plates, spoon the sauce over them and serve immediately. The dish may be accompanied by a mixed lettuce salad if you like.

Fish Rolls Energy 528kcal/2213kJ; Protein 45.9g; Carbohydrate 24.6g, of which sugars 2.8g; Fat 28.1g, of which saturates 11g; Cholesterol 142mg; Calcium 189mg; Fibre 1.3g; Sodium 1100mg.
Salmon 743kcal/3078kJ; Protein 43.3g; Carbohydrate 2.2g, of which sugars 2g; Fat 60.3g, of which saturates 27.8g; Cholesterol 198mg; Calcium 153mg; Fibre 0.6g; Sodium 164mg.

Cod Creole

Inspired by the cuisine of the Caribbean, this lightly spiced fish dish is both colourful and delicious, as well as being quick and easy to prepare.

Serves 4

450g/1lb cod fillets
15ml/1 tbsp lime or lemon juice
10ml/2 tsp olive oil
1 onion, finely chopped
1 green (bell) pepper, seeded and sliced
2.5ml/½ tsp cayenne pepper
2.5ml/½ tsp garlic salt
425g/14oz can chopped tomatoes
boiled rice or potatoes, to serve

1 Skin the cod fillets if this has not already been done by your fish supplier, then cut the flesh into bitesize chunks and sprinkle with the lime or lemon juice.

2 Heat the oil in a large, non-stick frying pan over low heat. Add the onion and green pepper and cook, stirring occasionally, for about 5 minutes, until softened. Add the cayenne pepper and garlic salt.

3 Stir in the cod and the chopped tomatoes, increase the heat to medium and bring to the boil. Lower the heat, cover and simmer for about 5 minutes, or until the fish flakes easily. Transfer the fish and sauce to warmed plates and serve immediately with boiled rice or potatoes.

Cook's Tip

This flavoursome dish is surprisingly light in calories and low in fat, so if you are worried about your waistline or conscientious about a healthy diet, this would be an excellent choice. In addition, (bell) peppers are a good source of vitamin C, while tomatoes are rich in the antioxidant lycopene, which is thought to lower the risk of some cancers. Processed and cooked tomatoes – in this case, canned tomatoes – are an even richer source because processing or cooking them makes it easier for the body to absorb lycopene.

Sea Bass en Papillote

Bring the unopened parcels to the table and let your guests uncover their own fish to release the delicious aroma of this dish.

Serves 4

4 small sea bass, scaled, gutted and with fins trimmed
130g/4½oz/generous ½ cup butter
450g/1lb spinach, coarse stalks removed
3 shallots, finely chopped
60ml/4 tbsp white wine
4 bay leaves
salt and ground black pepper

1 Preheat the oven to 180°C/350°F/Gas 4. Season both the inside and outside of the fish with salt and pepper.

2 Melt 50g/2oz/4 tbsp of the butter in a large, heavy pan over low heat. Add the spinach and cook gently, turning once or twice, until the spinach has broken down into a smooth purée. Remove from the heat and set aside to cool.

3 Melt another 50g/2oz/4 tbsp of the butter in a clean pan over low heat. Add the shallots and cook, stirring occasionally, for 5 minutes, until soft. Add to the spinach and leave to cool, then divide the spinach mixture among the cavities of the fish.

4 For each fish, fold a large sheet of greaseproof (waxed) paper in half, lay the fish on one half and cut around it to make a heart shape when opened out. The paper should be at least 5cm/2in larger all round than the fish. Remove the fish from the paper hearts.

5 Melt the remaining butter and brush a little on to the paper. Replace the fish and add 15ml/1 tbsp wine and a bay leaf to each parcel. Fold the other side of the paper over the fish and make small pleats to seal the two edges, starting at the curve of the heart. Brush the outsides with butter.

5 Transfer the parcels to a baking sheet and bake for 20–25 minutes, until the parcels are brown. Lift the parcels on to warmed plates with a metal spatula and serve immediately.

Cod Energy 144kcal/607kJ; Protein 22.1g; Carbohydrate 7.9g, of which sugars 7.4g; Fat 2.9g, of which saturates 0.5g; Cholesterol 52mg; Calcium 26mg; Fibre 2.2g; Sodium 81mg.
Sea Bass Energy 446kcal/1850kJ; Protein 35.2g; Carbohydrate 2.3g, of which sugars 2.1g; Fat 31.8g, of which saturates 17.7g; Cholesterol 201mg; Calcium 414mg; Fibre 2.4g; Sodium 469mg..

Spanish-style Hake

Hugely popular in Spain, hake is an unfairly neglected fish in many other countries.

Serves 4

30ml/2 tbsp olive oil
25g/1oz/2 tbsp butter
1 onion, chopped
3 garlic cloves, crushed
15g/½oz/1 tbsp plain (all-purpose) flour
2.5ml/½ tsp paprika
4 hake steaks (about 175g/6oz each)
250g/8oz fine green beans, cut into 2.5cm/1in lengths
350ml/12fl oz/1½ cups fresh fish stock
150ml/¼ pint/⅔ cup dry white wine
30ml/2 tbsp dry sherry
15–20 live mussels, scrubbed and debearded
45ml/3 tbsp chopped fresh parsley
salt and ground black pepper
crusty bread, to serve

1 Heat the oil and butter in a sauté or frying pan over low heat. Add the onion and cook, stirring occasionally, for about 5 minutes, until softened but not coloured. Add the garlic and cook for 1 minute more.

2 Mix together the flour and paprika, then lightly dust the hake with the mixture, shaking off any excess. Push the sautéed onion and garlic to one side of the pan.

3 Add the hake steaks to the pan and cook until golden on both sides. Stir in the beans, stock, wine and sherry and season to taste with salt and pepper. Bring to the boil and cook for about 2 minutes.

4 Discard any mussels with broken shells or that do not shut immediately when sharply tapped. Add the mussels and parsley to the pan, cover with a tight-fitting lid and cook for 5–8 minutes, until the mussels have opened. Discard any mussels that have remained closed.

5 Divide the hake, mussels and vegetables among warmed, shallow soup bowls and serve immediately with crusty bread to mop up the juices.

Mixed Smoked Fish Kedgeree

An ideal breakfast dish on a cold weekend morning and a classic for brunch. Garnish with quartered hard-boiled eggs and season well.

Serves 6

450g/1lb mixed smoked fish such as smoked cod, smoked haddock and smoked mussels or oysters
300ml/½ pint/1¼ cups milk
175g/6oz/scant 1 cup long grain rice
1 slice of lemon
50g/2oz/4 tbsp butter
5ml/1 tsp medium-hot curry powder
2.5ml/½ tsp freshly grated nutmeg
15ml/1 tbsp chopped fresh parsley
salt and ground black pepper
2 hard-boiled eggs, to garnish

1 Put the fish, but not the shellfish, in a large pan, add the milk and bring just to the boil. Lower the heat, cover and poach for 10 minutes, or until it flakes easily with the tip of a knife.

2 Remove the fish with a slotted spoon and set aside until cool enough to handle. Discard the milk. Remove the skin and any bones from the fish and flake the flesh. Mix with the smoked shellfish in a bowl and set aside.

3 Bring a pan of salted water to the boil, add the rice and slice of lemon and boil for 10 minutes, or according to the instructions on the packet, until just tender. Drain well and discard the lemon.

4 Melt the butter in a large frying pan and add the rice and fish. Shake the pan to mix all the ingredients together.

5 Stir in the curry powder, nutmeg, parsley and seasoning. Serve immediately, garnished with quartered eggs.

> **Cook's Tip**
> When flaking the fish, keep the pieces fairly large to give the dish a chunky consistency.

Hake Energy 338kcal/1409kJ; Protein 35.6g; Carbohydrate 6.9g, of which sugars 2.7g; Fat 15.2g, of which saturates 4.7g; Cholesterol 62mg; Calcium 68mg; Fibre 1.7g; Sodium 264mg.
Kedgeree Energy 250kcal/1044kJ; Protein 17.7g; Carbohydrate 25.8g, of which sugars 2.5g; Fat 8.3g, of which saturates 5g; Cholesterol 55mg; Calcium 79mg; Fibre 0.1g; Sodium 950mg.

Monkfish with Mexican Salsa

It is rare to see whole
monkfish on sale generally,
as only the tail is eaten.
Apart from its delicious
flavour and meaty texture,
the tail has the advantage of
having no pinbones.

Serves 4
675g/1½lb monkfish tail
45ml/3 tbsp olive oil
30ml/2 tbsp lime juice
1 garlic clove, crushed
15ml/1 tbsp chopped fresh
   coriander (cilantro)
salt and ground black pepper
fresh coriander sprigs and lime
   slices, to garnish

For the salsa
4 tomatoes, seeded, peeled
   and diced
1 avocado, stoned (pitted), peeled
   and diced
½ red onion, chopped
1 green chilli, seeded
   and chopped
30ml/2 tbsp chopped
   fresh coriander
30ml/2 tbsp olive oil
15ml/1 tbsp lime juice

1 To make the salsa, mix all the salsa ingredients and leave to
stand at room temperature for about 40 minutes.

2 Prepare the monkfish. Using a sharp knife, remove the
pinkish-grey membrane. Cut the fillets from either side of the
backbone, then cut each fillet in half to give four steaks.

3 Mix together the oil, lime juice, garlic and coriander in a
shallow non-metallic dish and season with salt and pepper. Turn
the monkfish several times to coat with the marinade, then
cover the dish and leave to marinate in a cool place or in the
refrigerator, for 30 minutes. Preheat the grill (broiler).

4 Remove the monkfish from the marinade and grill (broil) for
10–12 minutes, turning once and brushing frequently with the
marinade until cooked through.

5 Serve the monkfish garnished with coriander sprigs and lime
slices and accompanied by the salsa.

Seafood Crêpes

The combination of fresh
and smoked haddock
imparts a wonderful flavour
to the crêpe filling.

Serves 4–6
12 ready-made crêpes
melted butter, for brushing

For the filling
225g/8oz smoked haddock fillet
225g/8oz fresh haddock fillet

300ml/½ pint/1¼ cups milk
150ml/¼ pint/⅔ cup single
   (light) cream
40g/1½oz/3 tbsp butter
40g/1½oz/3 tbsp plain (all-
   purpose) flour
pinch of freshly grated nutmeg
2 hard-boiled eggs, shelled
   and chopped
salt and ground black pepper
sprinkling of Gruyère cheese and
   curly salad leaves, to serve

1 To make the filling, put the smoked and fresh haddock fillets
in a large pan, add the milk and bring just to the boil. Lower the
heat, cover and poach for 6–8 minutes, until just tender. Lift out
the fish with a slotted spoon and, when cool enough to handle,
remove the skin and bones. Reserve the milk. Pour the cream
into a measuring jug (cup), then strain enough milk into the jug
to make it up to 450ml/¾ pint/scant 2 cups.

2 Melt the butter in a pan over low heat. Stir in the flour and
cook, stirring constantly, for 1 minute. Gradually add the milk
mixture, stirring constantly to make a smooth sauce. Cook for
2–3 minutes. Season to taste with salt, pepper and nutmeg.
Flake the haddock and fold into the sauce with the eggs.
Remove the pan from the heat and leave to cool.

3 Preheat the oven to 180°C/350°F/Gas 4. Divide the filling
among the crêpes. Fold the sides of each crêpe into the centre,
then roll them up to enclose the filling completely. Brush four
or six individual ovenproof dishes with melted butter and
arrange two or three filled crêpes in each, or grease one large
dish for all the crêpes. Brush the crêpes with melted butter and
cook for 15 minutes.

4 Sprinkle over the Gruyère and cook for a further 5 minutes.
Serve hot with a few curly salad leaves.

Monkfish Energy 320kcal/1335kJ; Protein 31g; Carbohydrate 4.9g, of which sugars 4.2g; Fat 19.6g, of which saturates 3.3g; Cholesterol 27mg; Calcium 36mg; Fibre 2.3g; Sodium 46mg.
Seafood Energy 567kcal/2373kJ; Protein 24.9g; Carbohydrate 47.8g, of which sugars 20.1g; Fat 32.1g, of which saturates 7.1g; Cholesterol 118mg; Calcium 188mg; Fibre 1.2g; Sodium 445mg.

Smoked Trout Salad

Horseradish goes just as well with smoked trout as it does with roast beef. It combines well with yogurt to make a lovely dressing.

Serves 4

1 oak leaf or other red lettuce, such as lollo rosso
225g/8oz small ripe tomatoes, cut into thin wedges
½ cucumber, peeled and thinly sliced
4 smoked trout fillets, about 200g/7oz each, skinned and coarsely flaked

For the dressing
pinch of English (hot) mustard powder
15–20ml/3–4 tsp white wine vinegar
30ml/2 tbsp light olive oil
100ml/3½fl oz/scant ½ cup natural (plain) yogurt
about 30ml/2 tbsp grated fresh or bottled horseradish
pinch of caster (superfine) sugar

1 To make the dressing, mix together the mustard powder and vinegar in a bowl, then gradually whisk in the olive oil, yogurt, grated horseradish and sugar. Set aside in a cool place for about 30 minutes.

2 Place the lettuce leaves in a large bowl. Stir the dressing again, then pour half of it over the leaves and toss lightly using two spoons.

3 Arrange the lettuce on four individual plates with the tomatoes, cucumber and trout. Spoon the remaining dressing over the salads and serve immediately.

Cook's Tips
• The addition of salt to the horseradish salad dressing should not be necessary because of the saltiness of the smoked trout fillets.
• Look for natural, uncoloured smoked trout fillets – they should be a delicate cream colour.

Moroccan Fish Tagine

In Morocco *tagine* is the name of the large cooking pot used for this type of cooking, as well as the name of the dish.

Serves 4

2 garlic cloves, crushed
30ml/2 tbsp ground cumin
30ml/2 tbsp paprika
1 small fresh red chilli, seeded and finely chopped (optional)

30ml/2 tbsp tomato purée (paste)
60ml/4 tbsp lemon juice
4 whiting or cod steaks (about 175g/6oz each)
350g/12oz tomatoes, sliced
2 green (bell) peppers, seeded and thinly sliced
salt and ground black pepper
chopped fresh coriander (cilantro) or flat leaf parsley, to garnish

1 Mix together the garlic, cumin, paprika, chilli, if using, tomato purée and lemon juice in a bowl. Place the fish in a shallow dish and spread this mixture over it. Cover with clear film (plastic wrap) and chill in the refrigerator for about 30 minutes to let the flavours penetrate.

2 Preheat the oven to 200°C/400°F/Gas 6. Arrange half of the tomatoes and peppers in an ovenproof dish.

3 Cover with the fish, then arrange the remaining tomatoes and peppers on top. Cover the dish with foil and bake for about 45 minutes, until the fish is tender. Sprinkle with chopped coriander or parsley to serve.

Cook's Tips
• Try different white fish in this dish, such as hoki, hake, ling or pollack.
• If you are preparing this dish for a dinner party, it can be assembled completely and stored in the refrigerator until you are ready to cook it.
• Green (bell) peppers have a pleasing sharpness that goes well with this dish, but if you want to add more colour, substitute a red or yellow pepper for one of the green ones.

Trout Energy 303kcal/1268kJ; Protein 40.9g; Carbohydrate 4.4g, of which sugars 4.4g; Fat 13.7g, of which saturates 1g; Cholesterol 0mg; Calcium 81mg; Fibre 1g; Sodium 139mg.
Tagine Energy 174kcal/735kJ; Protein 33.7g; Carbohydrate 6.1g, of which sugars 5.9g; Fat 1.8g, of which saturates 0.4g; Cholesterol 81mg; Calcium 32mg; Fibre 2.5g; Sodium 135mg.

Mediterranean Fish Stew

Use any combination of white fish you like in this tasty stew.

Serves 4

225g/8oz/2 cups cooked prawns (shrimp) in the shell
450g/1lb mixed white fish fillets, skinned and chopped (reserve skins for the stock)
45ml/3 tbsp olive oil
1 onion, chopped
1 leek, sliced
1 carrot, diced
1 garlic clove, chopped
2.5ml/½ tsp ground turmeric
150ml/¼ pint/⅔ cup dry white wine or (hard) cider
400g/14oz can chopped tomatoes
sprig of fresh parsley, thyme and fennel
1 bay leaf
small piece of orange rind
1 prepared squid, body cut into rings and tentacles chopped
12 fresh mussels, scrubbed
salt and ground black pepper
30–45ml/2–3 tbsp fresh Parmesan cheese shavings and fresh parsley, to garnish

For the rouille sauce

2 slices white bread, crusts removed
2 garlic cloves, crushed
½ fresh red chilli
15ml/1 tbsp tomato purée (paste)
45–60ml/3–4 tbsp olive oil

1 Remove the heads and peel the prawns, leaving the tails intact. Reserve the shells and devein the prawns. Make a stock by simmering the prawn shells and fish skins in 450ml/¾ pint/scant 2 cups water for 20 minutes. Strain and reserve.

2 Heat the oil in a large pan. Add the onion, leek, carrot and garlic and cook, stirring occasionally, for 6–7 minutes. Stir in the turmeric and add the wine, tomatoes, reserved stock, herbs and orange rind. Bring to the boil, cover and simmer for 20 minutes.

3 To make the rouille sauce, process all the sauce ingredients in a food processor or blender.

4 Add the fish and seafood to the pan and simmer for 5–6 minutes, until the mussels open. Remove the bay leaf and rind and season to taste. Serve with a spoonful of the rouille, garnished with Parmesan cheese and parsley.

Salmon with Herb Butter

Other fresh herbs could be used to flavour the butter – try mint, fennel, flat leaf parsley or oregano.

Serves 4

50g/2oz/4 tbsp butter, softened, plus extra for greasing
finely grated rind of ½ small lemon
15ml/1 tbsp lemon juice
15ml/1 tbsp chopped fresh dill
4 salmon steaks
2 lemon slices, halved
4 fresh dill sprigs
salt and ground black pepper

1 Place the butter, lemon rind, lemon juice and chopped dill in a small bowl, season with salt and pepper and mix together with a fork until thoroughly blended.

2 Spoon the butter on to a piece of greaseproof (waxed) paper and roll up, smoothing with your hands into a neat sausage shape. Twist the ends of the paper tightly, wrap in clear film (plastic wrap) and place in the freezer for about 20 minutes, until firm.

3 Meanwhile, preheat the oven to 190°C/375°F/Gas 5. Cut out four squares of foil each big enough to enclose a salmon steak and grease lightly with butter. Place a salmon steak in the centre of each square.

4 Remove the herb butter from the freezer, unwrap and slice into eight rounds. Place two rounds on top of each salmon steak, then place a halved lemon slice in the centre and a sprig of dill on top. Lift up the edges of the foil and crinkle them together until they are well sealed.

5 Lift the parcels on to a baking sheet and bake for about 20 minutes, until the fish is cooked through. (Loosen the top of one parcel to check, if necessary.)

6 Remove from the oven and transfer the unopened parcels to warmed plates with a fish slice or metal spatula. Open the parcels and slide the contents on to the plates with the cooking juices. Serve immediately.

Fish Stew Energy 505kcal/2112kJ; Protein 51.7g; Carbohydrate 15.8g, of which sugars 7.8g; Fat 23.8g, of which saturates 5.4g; Cholesterol 349mg; Calcium 252mg; Fibre 3.1g; Sodium 520mg.
Salmon Energy 364kcal/1511kJ; Protein 30.5g; Carbohydrate 0.2g, of which sugars 0.1g; Fat 26.8g, of which saturates 9.4g; Cholesterol 102mg; Calcium 39mg; Fibre 0.1g; Sodium 144mg.

Spanish Seafood Paella

Use monkfish instead of the cod, if you like, and add a red mullet or snapper cut into chunks.

Serves 4

60ml/4 tbsp olive oil

225g/8oz cod, skinned and cut into chunks

3 prepared baby squid, body cut into rings and tentacles chopped

1 onion, chopped

3 garlic cloves, finely chopped

1 red (bell) pepper, seeded and sliced

4 tomatoes, peeled and chopped

225g/8oz/1¼ cups Valencia or risotto rice

450ml/¾ pint/scant 2 cups fish stock

150ml/¼ pint/⅔ cup dry white wine

75g/3oz/¼ cup frozen peas

4–5 saffron threads, soaked in 30ml/2 tbsp hot water

115g/4oz/1 cup cooked peeled prawns (shrimp)

8 fresh mussels, scrubbed and debearded

salt and ground black pepper

15ml/1 tbsp chopped fresh parsley, to garnish

lemon wedges, to serve

1 Heat 30ml/2 tbsp of the olive oil in a heavy frying pan over medium heat. Add the cod and squid and stir-fry for 2 minutes. Transfer to a bowl.

2 Heat the remaining oil in the pan over low heat. Add the onion, garlic and red pepper and cook, stirring occasionally, for 6–7 minutes, until softened but not coloured.

3 Stir in the tomatoes and cook for a further 2 minutes, then add the rice, stirring to coat the grains with oil, and cook for 2–3 minutes more. Pour in the fish stock and wine and add the peas and saffron with its soaking water. Season to taste with salt and pepper.

4 Gently stir in the reserved cooked fish with all the juices, followed by the prawns. Push the mussels into the rice. Cover with a tight-fitting lid and cook over low heat for about 30 minutes, or until the stock has been absorbed. Remove from the heat, keep covered and leave to stand for 5 minutes. Sprinkle with parsley and serve with lemon wedges.

Spaghetti with Seafood Sauce

The tomato-based sauce in this dish is a traditional marinara, popular in Italy's coastal regions.

Serves 4

45ml/3 tbsp olive oil

1 onion, chopped

1 garlic clove, finely chopped

225g/8oz spaghetti

600ml/1 pint/2½ cups passata (bottled strained tomatoes)

15ml/1 tbsp tomato purée (paste)

5ml/1 tsp dried oregano

1 bay leaf

5ml/1 tsp sugar

225g/8 oz/2 cups cooked peeled prawns (shrimp)

175g/6oz cooked clam or cockle meat (rinsed well if canned or bottled)

15ml/1 tbsp lemon juice

45ml/3 tbsp chopped fresh parsley

25g/1oz/2 tbsp butter

salt and ground black pepper

4 cooked prawns, to garnish

1 Heat the olive oil in a large pan over low heat. Add the onion and garlic and cook, stirring occasionally, for 6–7 minutes, until softened but not coloured.

2 Meanwhile, cook the spaghetti in a large pan of boiling salted water for 10–12 minutes, or according to the instructions on the packet, until just tender.

3 Stir the passata, tomato purée, oregano, bay leaf and sugar into the onion mixture and season to taste with salt and pepper. Bring to the boil, then simmer for 2–3 minutes.

4 Add the prawns, clams or cockles, lemon juice and 30ml/ 2 tbsp of the parsley. Stir well, then cover and cook for a further 6–7 minutes.

5 Drain the spaghetti, return to the pan and add the butter. Using two large spoons, toss well to coat, then season with salt and pepper.

6 Divide the spaghetti among four warmed plates and top with the seafood sauce. Sprinkle with the remaining parsley, garnish with whole prawns and serve immediately.

Paella Energy 478kcal/1998kJ; Protein 29.8g; Carbohydrate 53.1g, of which sugars 6.9g; Fat 13.4g, of which saturates 2g; Cholesterol 198mg; Calcium 74mg; Fibre 2.1g; Sodium 181mg.
Spaghetti Energy 414kcal/1749kJ; Protein 28.3g; Carbohydrate 48.8g, of which sugars 7.8g; Fat 13.2g, of which saturates 3.5g; Cholesterol 198mg; Calcium 131mg; Fibre 2.9g; Sodium 1818mg.

Grilled Fresh Sardines

Fresh sardines are flavoursome, firm-fleshed and rather different in taste and consistency from those canned in oil.

Serves 4–6
900kg/2lb fresh sardines, gutted
  and with heads removed
olive oil, for brushing
45ml/3 tbsp chopped
  fresh parsley
salt and ground black pepper
lemon wedges, to garnish

1 Preheat the grill (broiler). Rinse the sardines under cold running water. Pat dry with kitchen paper.

2 Brush the sardines lightly with olive oil and sprinkle generously with salt and pepper. Place the sardines in one layer in a grill (broiler) pan. Grill (broil) for about 3–4 minutes.

3 Turn, and cook for 3–4 minutes more, or until the skin begins to brown. Serve immediately, sprinkled with parsley and garnished with lemon wedges.

Cook's Tip
Frozen sardines are now available in supermarkets and will keep well in the freezer for six weeks. Thaw them in the refrigerator overnight. Scrape off the scales with your hands, working from tail to head, then use a sharp pointed knife to slit the belly, remove the innards and cut the heads off. For a fuller flavour and to make them less likely to fall apart when you turn them, you might like to leave them whole, as they do in some Mediterranean countries.

Variation
Substitute parsley butter for the fresh parsley. Simply beat chopped fresh parsley and lemon juice to taste into butter.

Red Mullet with Tomatoes

Red mullet is a popular fish in Italy, and in this recipe both its flavour and colour are accentuated.

Serves 4
4 red mullet or snapper (about
  175–200g/6–7oz each)
450g/1lb tomatoes, peeled, or
  400g/14oz can plum tomatoes
60ml/4 tbsp olive oil
60ml/4 tbsp finely chopped
  fresh parsley
2 garlic cloves, finely chopped
120ml/4fl oz/½ cup dry
  white wine
4 thin lemon slices, cut in half
salt and ground black pepper

1 Scale and gut the fish or ask your fish supplier to do this for you. Rinse well under cold running water and pat dry with kitchen paper.

2 Finely chop the tomatoes. Heat the oil in a pan or flameproof casserole large enough to hold the fish in one layer. Add the parsley and garlic, and cook, stirring, for 1 minute. Stir in the tomatoes and cook over medium heat, stirring occasionally, for 15–20 minutes. Season to taste with salt and pepper.

3 Add the fish to the tomato sauce and cook over medium to high heat for 5 minutes. Add the wine and the lemon slices. Bring the sauce back to the boil and cook for about 5 minutes more. Turn the fish over and cook for a further 4–5 minutes, until the fish flakes easily. Transfer the fish to a warmed serving platter and keep warm until required.

4 Boil the sauce for 3–4 minutes to reduce it slightly, then spoon it over the fish and serve immediately.

Cook's Tip
The liver of red mullet is regarded as a delicacy so you can leave it intact when you gut the fish or ask your fish supplier to keep it for you. This does not apply if you are preparing this dish with red snapper.

Sardines Energy 214kcal/893kJ; Protein 23.4g; Carbohydrate 0.2g, of which sugars 0.2g; Fat 13.2g, of which saturates 3.2g; Cholesterol 0mg; Calcium 131mg; Fibre 0.4g; Sodium 130mg.
Red Mullet Energy 256kcal/1067kJ; Protein 20.4g; Carbohydrate 4g, of which sugars 3.9g; Fat 15.7g, of which saturates 1.7g; Cholesterol 0mg; Calcium 105mg; Fibre 1.7g; Sodium 115mg.

Middle Eastern Sea Bream

Buy the smallest sea bream you can find to cook whole, allowing a serving of one fish for two people.

Serves 4

1.75kg/4lb sea bream or porgy or 2 smaller sea bream or porgy
30ml/2 tbsp olive oil
75g/3oz/¾ cup pine nuts
1 large onion, finely chopped
450g/1lb ripe tomatoes, coarsely chopped
75g/3oz/½ cup raisins
2.5ml/½ tsp ground cinnamon
2.5ml/½ tsp mixed (apple pie) spice
45ml/3 tbsp chopped fresh mint
225g/8oz/generous 1 cup long grain rice
3 lemon slices
300ml/½ pint/1¼ cups fish stock

1 Trim the fins, scale the fish, then gut or ask your fish supplier to do this for you. Rinse well under cold running water and pat dry with kitchen paper. Meanwhile, preheat the oven to 175°C/350°F/Gas 4.

2 Heat the oil in a large, heavy pan over medium-low heat. Add the pine nuts and stir-fry for 1 minute. Add the onions and continue to stir-fry until softened but not coloured.

3 Add the tomatoes and simmer for 10 minutes, then stir in the raisins, half the cinnamon, half the mixed spice and the mint.

4 Add the rice and lemon slices. Transfer to a large roasting pan and pour the fish stock over the top.

5 Place the fish on top and cut several slashes in the skin. Sprinkle over a little salt, the remaining mixed spice and the remaining cinnamon and bake for 30–35 minutes for large fish or 20–25 minutes for smaller fish.

> **Variation**
> If you like, use almonds instead of pine nuts. Use the same quantity of blanched almonds and split them in half before stir-frying.

Salmon with Spicy Pesto

This pesto uses sunflower seeds and chilli as its flavouring rather than the classic basil and pine nuts.

Serves 4

4 salmon steaks (about 225g/8oz each)
30ml/2 tbsp sunflower oil
finely grated rind and juice of 1 lime
pinch of salt

For the pesto

6 mild fresh red chillies, seeded
2 garlic cloves
30ml/2 tbsp pumpkin or sunflower seeds
freshly grated rind and juice of 1 lime
75ml/5 tbsp olive oil
salt and ground black pepper

1 Insert a very sharp knife close to the top of the salmon's backbone. Working closely to the bone, cut your way to the end of the steak so one side of the steak has been released and one side is still attached. Repeat with the other side. Pull out any extra visible bones with a pair of tweezers.

2 Sprinkle a little salt on the surface and take hold of the end of the salmon, skin-side down. Insert a small sharp knife under the skin and, working away from you, cut off the skin, keeping as close to the skin as possible. Repeat with the three remaining pieces of fish.

3 Rub the sunflower oil into the boneless fish rounds and place in a non-metallic dish. Add the lime juice and rind, cover with clear film (plastic wrap) and place in the refrigerator to marinate for 2 hours.

4 To make the pesto, put the chillies, garlic, pumpkin or sunflower seeds, lime juice and rind in a food processor or blender and season with salt and pepper. Process until well mixed. With the motor running, gradually pour in the olive oil until the sauce has thickened and emulsified.

5 Preheat the grill (broiler). Drain the salmon from its marinade. Grill the fish steaks for about 5 minutes on each side and serve immediately with the spicy pesto.

Sea Bream Energy 562kcal/2348kJ; Protein 39.7g; Carbohydrate 46g, of which sugars 1.1g; Fat 24.1g, of which saturates 1.7g; Cholesterol 71mg; Calcium 89mg; Fibre 0.5g; Sodium 208mg.
Salmon Energy 653kcal/2719kJ; Protein 50.5g; Carbohydrate 1.4g, of which sugars 0.1g; Fat 49.6g, of which saturates 7.5g; Cholesterol 122mg; Calcium 60mg; Fibre 0.5g; Sodium 111mg.

Garlic Chilli Prawns

In Spain *gambas al ajillo* are traditionally cooked in small earthenware dishes, but a frying pan is just as suitable.

Serves 4
60ml/4 tbsp olive oil
2–3 garlic cloves, finely chopped
1/2 –1 fresh red chilli, seeded and chopped
16 cooked Mediterranean prawns (large shrimp)
15ml/1 tbsp chopped fresh parsley
salt and ground black pepper
lemon wedges and French bread, to serve

1 Heat the olive oil in a large frying pan over medium heat. Add the garlic and chilli and stir-fry for 1 minute, until the garlic begins to turn brown.

2 Add the prawns and stir-fry for 3–4 minutes, coating them well with the flavoured oil.

3 Add the parsley, remove from the heat and place four prawns in each of four warmed bowls. Spoon the flavoured oil over them. Serve with lemon wedges for squeezing and French bread to mop up the juices.

Tapas Prawns

These succulent prawns are simply irresistible as part of a *tapas* or *mezze*.

Serves 4
30ml/2 tbsp olive oil
4 garlic cloves, finely chopped
900g/2lb raw Mediteranean prawns (large shrimp), peeled
40g/1 1/2oz/3 tbsp butter
15ml/1 tbsp orange juice
chopped fresh parsley, to garnish

1 Heat the oil in a frying pan. Add the garlic cloves and cook for 1–2 minutes. Add the prawns and cook, turning gently, for 2 minutes. Stir in the butter and orange juice and cook until the prawns have changed colour. Sprinkle with chopped parsley.

Deep-fried Spicy Whitebait

This is a delicious British dish – serve these tiny fish very hot and crisp.

Serves 4
450g/1lb whitebait
40g/1 1/2oz/3 tbsp plain (all-purpose) flour
5ml/1 tsp paprika
pinch of cayenne pepper
12 fresh parsley sprigs
vegetable oil, for deep-frying
salt and ground black pepper
4 lemon wedges, to garnish

1 If using frozen whitebait, thaw in the bag, then drain off any water. Spread out the fish on kitchen paper and pat dry.

2 Place the flour, paprika and cayenne in a large plastic bag and add salt and pepper. Add the whitebait, in batches, and shake gently until all the fish are lightly coated with the flour mixture. Transfer to a plate.

3 Heat about 5cm/2in of oil in a pan or deep-fat fryer to 190°C/375°F, or until a cube of day-old bread browns in about 30 seconds.

4 Add the whitebait, in batches, and deep-fry in the hot oil for 2–3 minutes, until the coating is lightly golden and crisp. Remove from the pan with a slotted spoon, drain on kitchen paper and keep warm in the oven while frying the remainder.

5 When all the whitebait is cooked, drop the sprigs of parsley into the hot oil (don't worry if the oil spits slightly) and deep-fry for a few seconds until crisp. Drain on kitchen paper. Serve the whitebait immediately, garnished with the deep-fried parsley sprigs and lemon wedges.

> **Cook's Tip**
> There are two varieties of paprika, sweet and hot. Sweet paprika is quite mild, while hot paprika is spicier (but not as spicy as cayenne). Always check the label when buying.

Chilli Prawns Energy 157kcal/653kJ; Protein 13.3g; Carbohydrate 0.1g, of which sugars 0.1g; Fat 11.5g, of which saturates 1.7g; Cholesterol 146mg; Calcium 67mg; Fibre 0.2g; Sodium 144mg.
Tapas Prawns Energy 224kcal/928kJ; Protein 19.9g; Carbohydrate 1.4g, of which sugars 0.5g; Fat 15.3g, of which saturates 6.5g; Cholesterol 91mg; Calcium 127mg; Fibre 0.3g; Sodium 1434mg.
Whitebait Energy 591kcal/2446kJ; Protein 22g; Carbohydrate 6g, of which sugars 0.1g; Fat 53.5g, of which saturates 5g; Cholesterol 0mg; Calcium 968mg; Fibre 0.2g; Sodium 259mg.

Baked Fish Creole-style

Fish fillets cooked in a colourful pepper and tomato sauce are topped with a cheese crust.

Serves 4

15ml/1 tbsp sunflower oil
25g/1oz/2 tbsp butter, plus extra
   for greasing
1 onion, thinly sliced
1 garlic clove, chopped
1 red (bell) pepper, seeded, halved
   and sliced
1 green (bell) pepper, seeded,
   halved and sliced
400g/14oz can chopped
   tomatoes with basil

15ml/1 tbsp tomato
   purée (paste)
30ml/2 tbsp capers, drained
   and chopped
3–4 drops Tabasco sauce
4 tail end pieces cod or haddock
   fillets (about 175g/6oz
   each), skinned
6 basil leaves, shredded
45ml/3 tbsp fresh breadcrumbs
25g/1oz/¼ cup grated
   Cheddar cheese
10ml/2 tsp chopped fresh parsley
salt and ground black pepper
fresh basil sprigs, to garnish

1 Preheat the oven to 230°C/450°F/Gas 8. Heat the oil and half of the butter in a pan over low heat. Add the onion and cook, stirring occasionally, for about 6–7 minutes, until softened. Add the garlic, peppers, chopped tomatoes, tomato purée, capers and Tabasco and season to taste with salt and pepper. Cover and cook for 15 minutes, then uncover and simmer gently for 5 minutes to reduce slightly.

2 Grease an ovenproof dish, place the fish fillets in it, dot with the remaining butter and season lightly. Spoon the tomato and pepper sauce over the top and sprinkle with the shredded basil. Bake for about 10 minutes.

3 Meanwhile, mix together the breadcrumbs, cheese and parsley in a bowl. Remove the fish from the oven and sprinkle the cheese mixture over the top. Return to the oven and bake for about 10 minutes more. Let the fish stand for about a minute, then, using a fish slice or spatula, carefully transfer each topped fillet to warmed plates. Garnish with sprigs of fresh basil and serve immediately.

Tuna Fishcake Bites

An updated version of a traditional British tea-time dish, these delicious, little fishcakes would also make an elegant appetizer.

Serves 4

675g/1½lb potatoes
knob (pat) of butter
2 hard-boiled eggs, chopped
3 spring onions
   (scallions), chopped
grated rind of ½ lemon
5ml/1 tsp lemon juice
30ml/2 tbsp chopped
   fresh parsley
200g/7oz can tuna in oil, drained
10ml/2 tsp capers, drained
   and chopped

2 eggs, lightly beaten
115g/4oz/2 cups fresh
   white breadcrumbs
sunflower oil, for pan-frying
salt and ground black pepper
green salad, to serve

For the tartare sauce

60ml/4 tbsp mayonnaise
15ml/1 tbsp natural (plain) yogurt
15ml/1 tbsp finely
   chopped gherkins
15ml/1 tbsp capers, drained
   and chopped
15ml/1 tbsp chopped
   fresh parsley

1 Cook the potatoes in boiling salted water for 25–30 minutes, until tender. Drain and mash with the butter.

2 Mix the hard-boiled eggs, spring onions, lemon rind and juice, parsley, tuna, capers and 15ml/1 tbsp of the beaten eggs into the cooled potato. Season to taste, then cover and chill.

3 Mix all the sauce ingredients together. Chill in the refrigerator.

4 Roll the fishcake mixture into about 24 balls. Dip these into the remaining beaten eggs and then roll gently in the breadcrumbs until evenly coated. Transfer to a plate.

5 Heat 90ml/6 tbsp of the oil in a frying pan. Add the fish balls, in batches, and cook over medium heat, turning two or three times, for about 4 minutes, until browned all over. Drain on kitchen paper and keep warm in the oven while frying the remainder. Serve with the tartare sauce and a salad.

Baked Fish Energy 332kcal/1399kJ; Protein 38.1g; Carbohydrate 19.2g, of which sugars 10.2g; Fat 11.9g, of which saturates 5.4g; Cholesterol 82mg; Calcium 106mg; Fibre 3g; Sodium 308mg.
Fishcake Energy 567kcal/2380kJ; Protein 26.8g; Carbohydrate 54.5g, of which sugars 7.5g; Fat 28.4g, of which saturates 3.8g; Cholesterol 228mg; Calcium 111mg; Fibre 3g; Sodium 656mg.

Kashmir Coconut Fish Curry

The combination of spices in this dish give an interesting depth of flavour to the creamy curry sauce.

Serves 4

30ml/2 tbsp vegetable oil
2 onions, sliced
1 green (bell) pepper, seeded and sliced
1 garlic clove, crushed
1 dried chilli, seeded and chopped
5ml/1 tsp ground coriander
5ml/1 tsp ground cumin
2.5ml/½ tsp ground turmeric
2.5ml/½ tsp hot chilli powder
2.5ml/½ tsp garam masala
15g/½oz/1 tbsp plain (all-purpose) flour
300ml/½ pint/1¼ cups coconut cream
675g/1½lb haddock fillet, skinned and chopped
4 tomatoes, peeled, seeded and chopped
15ml/1 tbsp lemon juice
30ml/2 tbsp ground almonds
30ml/2 tbsp double (heavy) cream
fresh coriander (cilantro) sprigs, to garnish
naan bread and boiled rice, to serve

1 Heat the oil in a large pan over low heat. Add the onions, green pepper and garlic and cook, stirring occasionally, for 6–7 minutes, until the onions and pepper have softened but not coloured.

2 Stir in the dried chilli, ground coriander, cumin, turmeric, chilli powder, garam masala and flour and cook, stirring constantly, for 1 minute more.

3 Mix the coconut cream with 300ml/½ pint/1¼ cups boiling water and stir into the spicy vegetable mixture. Bring to the boil, cover with a tight-fitting lid and simmer gently for about 6 minutes.

4 Add the pieces of fish and the tomatoes, re-cover the pan and cook for 5–6 minutes, or until the fish has turned opaque and flakes easily with the tip of a knife. Uncover and gently stir in the lemon juice, ground almonds and cream and heat through for a few minutes. Season well, garnish with coriander and serve with naan bread and rice.

Mussels with Wine & Garlic

This famous French dish is traditionally known as *moules marinière*, and can be served as an appetizer or a main course.

Serves 4

1.75kg/4lb fresh mussels
15ml/1 tbsp olive oil
25g/1oz/2 tbsp butter
1 small onion or 2 shallots, finely chopped
2 garlic cloves, finely chopped
150ml/¼ pint/⅔ cup dry white wine
4 fresh parsley sprigs
ground black pepper
30ml/2 tbsp chopped fresh parsley, to garnish
French bread, to serve

1 Scrub the mussels under cold running water and pull off the beards. Discard any with broken shells or that do not shut immediately when sharply tapped.

2 Heat the oil and butter in a large pan over medium heat. Add the onion or shallots and garlic and cook, stirring occasionally, for 3–4 minutes.

3 Pour in the wine, add the parsley sprigs, stir well and bring to the boil. Add the mussels, cover with a tight-fitting lid and cook, shaking the pan occasionally, for 5–7 minutes, until the shells have opened. Discard any mussels that remain closed.

4 Transfer the mussels to warmed serving bowls with a slotted spoon. Strain the cooking juices through a fine strainer lined with muslin (cheesecloth) and spoon them over the shellfish. Sprinkle with the chopped parsley, season well with pepper and serve immediately with hot French bread.

Variation
This dish is served everywhere in France, but in the apple-growing region of Normandy it is made with (hard) cider rather than white wine. For a really rich dish, strain the cooking liquid into a pan, stir in 90ml/6 tbsp double (heavy) cream and cook for a few minutes before spooning over the mussels.

Curry Energy 496kcal/2068kJ; Protein 36.6g; Carbohydrate 18.9g, of which sugars 13.6g; Fat 31.1g, of which saturates 20.5g; Cholesterol 71mg; Calcium 75mg; Fibre 3.2g; Sodium 137mg.
Mussels Energy 224kcal/939kJ; Protein 20g; Carbohydrate 5.4g, of which sugars 1.1g; Fat 11g, of which saturates 4g; Cholesterol 83mg; Calcium 70mg; Fibre 0.2g; Sodium 460mg.

Thai Prawn Salad

This salad has the distinctive flavour of lemon grass, the bulbous grass used widely in South-east Asian cooking.

Serves 2

250g/9oz extra-large tiger prawns (jumbo shrimp), thawed if frozen
30ml/2 tbsp groundnut (peanut) oil
15ml/1 tbsp Thai fish sauce
30ml/2 tbsp lime juice
7.5ml/1 ½ tsp soft light brown sugar
1 small fresh red chilli, finely chopped
1 spring onion (scallion), finely chopped
1 small garlic clove, crushed
2.5cm/1in piece fresh lemon grass, finely chopped
30ml/2 tbsp chopped fresh coriander (cilantro)
45ml/3 tbsp dry white wine
8–12 Little Gem (Bibb) lettuce leaves, to serve
fresh coriander sprigs, to garnish

1 Remove the heads and peel the prawns. (Reserve the shells for making shellfish stock, if you like.) Make a shallow cut along the back of each prawn and remove the dark vein with the tip of the knife.

2 Heat the oil in a wok or heavy frying pan over medium heat. When it is very hot, add the prawns and stir-fry for 2–3 minutes, until they have changed colour. Be careful not to overcook them. Remove with a slotted spoon and drain on kitchen paper. Leave to cool.

3 Place the tiger prawns in a non-metallic bowl and add all the remaining ingredients except the lettuce and coriander sprigs. Stir thoroughly to combine and dissolve the sugar, cover with clear film (plastic wrap) and leave to marinate in the refrigerator for 2–3 hours, occasionally stirring and turning the prawns.

4 Arrange two or three of the lettuce leaves on each of four individual serving plates. Spoon the prawn salad and marinade on to the lettuce leaves. Garnish with fresh coriander sprigs and serve immediately.

Cajun Spiced Fish

Fillets of fish are coated with an aromatic blend of herbs and spices and pan-fried in butter.

Serves 4

5ml/1 tsp dried thyme
5ml/1 tsp dried oregano
5ml/1 tsp ground black pepper
1.25ml/¼ tsp cayenne pepper
10ml/2 tsp paprika
2.5ml/½ tsp garlic salt
4 tail end pieces of cod fillet (about 175g/6oz each)
75g/3oz/6 tbsp butter
½ fresh red (bell) pepper, seeded and sliced
½ green (bell) pepper, seeded and sliced
fresh thyme sprigs, to garnish
grilled (broiled) tomatoes and sweet potato purée, to serve

1 Place the dried thyme, oregano, black pepper, cayenne, paprika and garlic salt in a bowl and mix well. Dip the fish fillets in the spice mixture until lightly coated.

2 Heat 25g/1oz/2 tbsp of the butter in a large frying pan over medium-low heat. Add the red and green peppers and cook, stirring occasionally, for 4–5 minutes, until softened. Remove the peppers and keep warm.

3 Add the remaining butter to the pan and heat until it is sizzling. Add the cod fillets and cook over medium heat for 3–4 minutes on each side, until browned and cooked.

4 Transfer the fish to a warmed serving dish, surround with the peppers and garnish with thyme sprigs. Serve the spiced fish with some grilled tomatoes and sweet potato purée.

> ### Cook's Tip
> Cajun cooking is a rural tradition that originated in Louisiana over 200 years ago. It is an immensely flexible cuisine based on home-grown crops, locally caught fish and any game that could be hunted. It is often confused with Creole cuisine, which evolved in the same region but was created for the rich. Creole includes French, Spanish and African influences.

Thai Prawn Energy 130kcal/546kJ; Protein 22.4g; Carbohydrate 4.7g, of which sugars 4.6g; Fat 0.9g, of which saturates 0.2g; Cholesterol 244mg; Calcium 112mg; Fibre 0.3g; Sodium 240mg.
Cajun Fish Energy 295kcal/1228kJ; Protein 32.7g; Carbohydrate 3g, of which sugars 2.9g; Fat 16.9g, of which saturates 10g; Cholesterol 120mg; Calcium 31mg; Fibre 0.9g; Sodium 222mg.

Tuna, Anchovy & Caper Pizza

Packed with Italian flavours, this substantial pizza is great for an informal gathering.

Serves 2–3
115g/4oz/1 cup self- raising (self-rising) flour
115g/4oz/1 cup self-raising wholemeal (self-rising whole-wheat) flour
pinch of salt
50g/2oz/¼ cup butter, diced
about 150ml/¼ pint/⅔ cup milk

For the topping
30ml/2 tbsp olive oil
1 jar ready-made tomato sauce or pizza topping
1 small red onion
200g/7oz can tuna, drained
15ml/1 tbsp capers
12 black olives, pitted
45ml/3 tbsp freshly grated Parmesan cheese
50g/2oz can anchovy fillets, drained and halved lengthways
ground black pepper

1 Place the flours and salt in a bowl and rub in the butter until the mixture resembles fine breadcrumbs. Add the milk and mix to a soft dough with a wooden spoon. Knead on a lightly floured surface until smooth.

2 Preheat the oven to 220°C/425°F/Gas 7. Roll out the dough on a lightly floured surface to a 25cm/10in circle. Place on a greased baking sheet and brush with 15ml/1 tbsp of the oil. Spread the tomato sauce or pizza topping evenly over the dough, leaving the edge uncovered.

3 Cut the onion into thin wedges and arrange on top. Roughly flake the tuna with a fork and scatter over the onion. Sprinkle over the capers, black olives and Parmesan cheese.

4 Place the anchovy fillets over the top of the pizza in a criss-cross pattern. Drizzle over the remaining oil, then grind over plenty of pepper. Bake for 15–20 minutes until crisp and golden. Serve immediately.

> **Variation**
> If you have time, make your own herb-flavoured tomato sauce.

Salmon & Avocado Pizza

Smoked and fresh salmon make a delicious and luxurious pizza topping when mixed with avocado.

Serves 3–4
150g/5oz salmon fillet
120ml/4fl oz/½ cup dry white wine
1 quantity Basic Pizza Dough (see page 158)
15ml/1 tbsp olive oil
400g/14oz can chopped tomatoes, drained well

115g/4oz/scant 1 cup grated mozzarella
1 small avocado
10ml/2 tsp lemon juice
30ml/2 tbsp crème fraîche
75g/3oz smoked salmon, cut into strips
15ml/1 tbsp capers
30ml/2 tbsp snipped fresh chives, to garnish
ground black pepper

1 Place the salmon fillet in a frying pan, pour over the wine and season with pepper. Bring slowly to the boil over gentle heat, remove from the heat, cover with a tight-fitting lid and leave to cool. (The fish will cook in the cooling liquid.) Skin and flake the salmon into small pieces, removing any bones.

2 Preheat the oven to 220°C/425°F/Gas 7. Roll out the pizza dough to a 25–30cm/10–12in circle and place on a greased baking sheet. Push up the edge of the dough to form a thin rim.

3 Brush the pizza base with the oil and spread the drained tomatoes over the top. Sprinkle half the mozzarella. Bake for 10 minutes, then remove from the oven.

4 Meanwhile, halve, stone and peel the avocado. Cut the flesh into small dice and toss in the lemon juice.

5 Dot teaspoonfuls of the crème fraîche over the pizza base. Arrange the fresh and smoked salmon, avocado, capers and remaining mozzarella on top. Season to taste with pepper.

6 Bake for 5–10 minutes until crisp and golden. Sprinkle over the chives and serve immediately.

Tuna Energy 713kcal/2985kJ; Protein 37.8g; Carbohydrate 58.5g, of which sugars 3.8g; Fat 38.1g, of which saturates 15g; Cholesterol 97mg; Calcium 328mg; Fibre 5.7g; Sodium 1518mg.
Salmon Energy 451kcal/1884kJ; Protein 22g; Carbohydrate 31g, of which sugars 5.3g; Fat 25.3g, of which saturates 8.6g; Cholesterol 53mg; Calcium 193mg; Fibre 3.3g; Sodium 282mg.

Tagliatelle with Saffron Mussels

Mussels bathed in a delicate saffron and cream sauce are served with tagliatelle for a simple, yet sophisticated, lunch or supper dish.

Serves 4

1.8kg/4–4¹/₂lb live mussels in the shell
150ml/¹/₄ pint/²/₃ cup dry white wine
2 shallots, finely chopped
350g/12oz dried tagliatelle
25g/1oz/2 tbsp butter
2 garlic cloves, crushed
250ml/8fl oz/1 cup double (heavy) cream
large pinch of saffron threads
1 egg yolk
salt and ground black pepper
30ml/2 tbsp chopped fresh parsley, to garnish

1 Scrub the mussels well under cold running water. Remove the "beards" and discard any mussels that are open.

2 Place the mussels in a large pan with the white wine and chopped shallots. Cover with a tight-fitting lid and cook over high heat for 5–8 minutes, shaking the pan occasionally, until the mussels have opened.

3 Drain the mussels, reserving the cooking liquid. Discard any mussels that remain closed. Shell all but a few of the mussels and keep warm. Bring the reserved cooking liquid to the boil, then reduce by half. Strain into a jug (cup).

4 Bring a large pan of lightly salted water to the boil and cook the tagliatelle for 10 minutes or until *al dente*.

5 Meanwhile, melt the butter in a frying pan and fry the garlic for 1 minute. Pour in the reduced mussel liquid, cream and saffron threads. Heat gently until the sauce thickens slightly.

6 Remove the pan from the heat and stir in the egg yolk and shelled mussels. Season to taste with salt and pepper.

7 Drain the tagliatelle and transfer to warmed serving bowls. Spoon the sauce over and sprinkle with chopped parsley. Garnish with the mussels in shells and serve immediately.

Pasta with Prawns & Feta Cheese

Pasta tubes tossed with fresh prawns and sharp-tasting feta cheese is a winning combination. Serve with a mixed salad for an impressive light meal.

Serves 4

450g/1lb/4 cups medium raw prawns (shrimp)
6 spring onions (scallions)
50g/2oz/4 tbsp butter
225g/8oz feta cheese
small bunch fresh chives
450g/1lb/4 cups dried penne, garganelle or rigatoni
salt and ground black pepper

1 Remove the heads from the prawns by twisting and pulling off. Peel the prawns and discard the shells. With a sharp knife, remove the black intestinal vein running down the back of larger prawns and discard. Chop the spring onions.

2 Melt the butter in a frying pan and cook the prawns until they turn pink, then add the spring onions and cook gently for a further 1 minute.

3 Cut the feta cheese into 1cm/¹/₂in dice. Stir the cheese into the prawn mixture and season to taste with pepper.

4 Cut the chives into 2.5cm/1in lengths and stir half into the prawn mixture.

5 Bring a large pan of lightly salted water to the boil and cook the pasta until *al dente*. Drain well, pile into a warmed serving dish and top with the sauce. Scatter with the remaining chives and serve immediately.

Cook's Tips
• Substitute goat's cheese for the feta cheese if you like; prepare the dish in the same way.
• If raw prawns are unavailable, use cooked prawns but cook the spring onions first, then add the prawns to heat through.

Tagliatelle Energy 803kcal/3366kJ; Protein 34.8g; Carbohydrate 67.6g, of which sugars 5.3g; Fat 43.1g, of which saturates 24.7g; Cholesterol 152mg; Calcium 339mg; Fibre 3.3g; Sodium 335mg.
Prawns & Feta Energy 707kcal/2980kJ; Protein 42.5g; Carbohydrate 84.7g, of which sugars 5.1g; Fat 24.4g, of which saturates 14.6g; Cholesterol 285mg; Calcium 328mg; Fibre 3.5g; Sodium 1104mg.

Honey & Orange Glazed Chicken

This dish is popular in the United States and Australia and is ideal for an easy meal served with baked potatoes.

Serves 4
4 boneless chicken breast portions (about 175g/6oz each)
15ml/1 tbsp sunflower oil
4 spring onions (scallions), chopped
1 garlic clove, crushed
45ml/3 tbsp clear honey
60ml/4 tbsp fresh orange juice
1 orange, peeled and segmented
30ml/2 tbsp soy sauce
fresh lemon balm or flat leaf parsley, to garnish
baked potatoes and mixed salad, to serve

1 Preheat the oven to 190°C/375°F/Gas 5. Place the chicken portions, with skin still on, in a single layer in a shallow roasting pan and set aside.

2 Heat the sunflower oil in a small pan over low heat. Add the spring onions and garlic and cook, stirring occasionally, for about 2 minutes, until softened but not coloured.

3 Add the honey, orange juice, orange segments and soy sauce to the pan and cook, stirring constantly, until the honey has completely dissolved.

4 Pour the sauce over the chicken and bake, uncovered, for about 45 minutes, until the chicken is cooked, basting once or twice with the cooking juices. Check by piercing the thickest part with the point of a knife; the juices should run clear. Transfer the chicken to warmed individual plates, garnish with lemon balm or flat leaf parsley and serve immediately with baked potatoes and a salad.

> **Variation**
> Create a slightly spicier version of this dish by substituting the same quantity of honey-flavoured mustard for the clear honey. Ensure the mustard has dissolved completely.

Italian Chicken

Use chicken legs, breast portions or quarters in this colourful dish, and a different type of ribbon pasta if you like.

Serves 4
25g/1oz/¼ cup plain (all-purpose) flour
4 chicken portions
30ml/2 tbsp olive oil
1 onion, chopped
2 garlic cloves, chopped
1 red (bell) pepper, seeded and chopped
400g/14oz can chopped tomatoes
30ml/2 tbsp red pesto sauce
4 sun-dried tomatoes in oil, drained and chopped
150ml/¼ pint/⅔ cup chicken stock
5ml/1 tsp dried oregano
8 black olives, pitted
salt and ground black pepper
chopped fresh basil and whole basil leaves, to garnish
tagliatelle, to serve

1 Place the flour in a plastic bag and season with salt and pepper. Add the chicken portions and shake well until they are coated. Heat the oil in a flameproof casserole over medium heat. Add the chicken portions and cook, turning frequently, for 8–10 minutes, until browned all over. Remove with a slotted spoon and set aside.

2 Lower the heat, add the onion, garlic and red pepper and cook, stirring occasionally, for 5 minutes, until the onion is softened but not coloured.

3 Stir in the canned tomatoes, red pesto, sun-dried tomatoes, stock and oregano and bring to the boil.

4 Return the chicken portions to the casserole, season lightly with salt and pepper, cover with a tight-fitting lid and simmer gently for 30–35 minutes, until the chicken is cooked.

5 Add the black olives and simmer for a further 5 minutes. Transfer the chicken and vegetables to a warmed serving dish, sprinkle with the chopped basil and garnish with whole basil leaves. Serve immediately with hot tagliatelle.

Italian Chicken Energy 515kcal/2181kJ; Protein 51.6g; Carbohydrate 44.3g, of which sugars 39.1g; Fat 16g, of which saturates 3.5g; Cholesterol 162mg; Calcium 110mg; Fibre 12.7g; Sodium 345mg.
Glazed Chicken Energy 251kcal/1062kJ; Protein 42.4g; Carbohydrate 10.5g, of which sugars 10.5g; Fat 4.7g, of which saturates 0.9g; Cholesterol 123mg; Calcium 12mg; Fibre 0g; Sodium 642mg.

Creole Chicken Jambalaya

Clearly influenced by Spanish paella, this New Orleans speciality is probably the best-known dish of Creole cuisine.

Serves 4

1.2kg/2½lb fresh chicken
1½ onions
1 bay leaf
4 black peppercorns
30ml/2 tbsp vegetable oil
2 garlic cloves, chopped
1 green (bell) pepper, seeded and chopped
1 celery stick, chopped
225g/8oz/1¼ cups long grain rice
115g/4oz chorizo sausage, sliced
115g/4oz/1 cup chopped cooked ham
400g/14oz can chopped tomatoes
2.5ml/½ tsp hot chilli powder
2.5ml/½ tsp cumin seeds
2.5ml/½ tsp ground cumin
5ml/1 tsp dried thyme
115g/4oz/1 cup cooked peeled prawns (shrimp)
dash of Tabasco sauce
salt and ground black pepper
chopped fresh parsley, to garnish

1 Place the chicken in a flameproof casserole and pour in 600ml/1 pint/2½ cups water. Add half an onion, the bay leaf and peppercorns and bring to the boil. Lower the heat, cover and simmer for 1½ hours. Then lift the chicken out of the pan. Remove and discard the skin and bones and chop the meat. Strain the stock and reserve.

2 Chop the remaining whole onion. Heat the oil in a large frying pan over low heat. Add the onion, garlic, green pepper and celery and cook, stirring occasionally, for 5 minutes. Stir in the rice. Add the chorizo, ham and chicken and cook, stirring frequently, for 2–3 minutes.

3 Pour in the tomatoes and 300ml/½ pint/1¼ cups of the reserved stock and add the chilli, cumin and thyme. Bring to the boil, cover and simmer gently for 20 minutes, or until the rice is tender and the liquid absorbed.

4 Stir in the prawns and Tabasco. Cook for 5 minutes more, then season to taste with salt and pepper. Serve immediately, garnished with chopped fresh parsley.

Moroccan Chicken Couscous

The combination of sweet and spicy flavours in the sauce and couscous makes this dish irresistible.

Serves 4

15g/½oz/1 tbsp butter
15ml/1 tbsp sunflower oil
4 chicken portions
2 onions, finely chopped
2 garlic cloves, crushed
2.5ml/½ tsp ground cinnamon
1.5ml/¼ tsp ground ginger
1.5ml/¼ tsp ground turmeric
30ml/2 tbsp orange juice
10ml/2 tsp clear honey
salt
fresh mint sprigs, to garnish

For the couscous

350g/12oz/2¼ cups couscous
5ml/1 tsp salt
10ml/2 tsp caster (superfine) sugar
15ml/1 tbsp sunflower oil
2.5ml/½ tsp ground cinnamon
pinch of grated nutmeg
15ml/1 tbsp orange blossom water
30ml/2 tbsp sultanas (golden raisins)
50g/2oz/½ cup chopped toasted almonds
45ml/3 tbsp chopped pistachios

1 Heat the butter and oil in a large pan over medium heat. Add the chicken portions, skin-side down, and cook, turning frequently, for 5–6 minutes, until golden. Turn them over. Add the onions, garlic, spices, a pinch of salt, the orange juice and 300ml/½ pint/1¼ cups water. Cover and bring to the boil, then lower the heat and simmer for about 30 minutes.

2 Mix the couscous with the salt and 350ml/12fl oz/1½ cups water in a bowl. Leave for 5 minutes. Add the rest of the ingredients for the couscous.

3 Line a steamer with baking parchment and spoon in the couscous. Set the steamer over the pan of chicken and steam for 10 minutes.

4 Remove the steamer and keep covered. Stir the honey into the chicken liquid and boil rapidly for 3–4 minutes. Serve the chicken on a bed of couscous with some sauce spooned over it. Garnish with fresh mint and serve with the remaining sauce.

Jambalaya Energy 802kcal/3340kJ; Protein 50.4g; Carbohydrate 59g, of which sugars 10.5g; Fat 40.5g, of which saturates 11.3g; Cholesterol 250mg; Calcium 104mg; Fibre 2.9g; Sodium 785mg.
Chicken Couscous Energy 630kcal/2639kJ; Protein 51.4g; Carbohydrate 64.1g, of which sugars 16.5g; Fat 20.2g, of which saturates 4.2g; Cholesterol 170mg; Calcium 91mg; Fibre 2.5g; Sodium 169mg.

Tandoori Chicken Kebabs

This popular dish originates from the Punjab, where it is traditionally cooked in clay ovens known as *tandoors*.

Serves 4

4 skinless chicken breast fillets
  (about 175g/6oz each)
15ml/1 tbsp lemon juice
45ml/3 tbsp tandoori paste
45ml/3 tbsp natural (plain) yogurt
1 garlic clove, crushed
30ml/2 tbsp chopped fresh
  coriander (cilantro)
1 small onion, cut into wedges
  and separated into layers
vegetable oil, for brushing
salt and ground black pepper
fresh coriander sprigs, to garnish
pilau rice and naan bread,
  to serve

1 Chop the chicken fillets into 2.5cm/1in dice and place in a bowl. Add the lemon juice, tandoori paste, yogurt, garlic and coriander and season with salt and pepper. Cover with clear film (plastic wrap) and leave to marinate in the refrigerator, stirring occasionally, for 2–3 hours.

2 Preheat the grill (broiler). Thread alternate pieces of marinated chicken and onion on to four skewers.

3 Brush the onions with a little oil, lay on a grill (broiler) rack and cook under high heat for 10–12 minutes, turning once. Transfer the skewers to warmed plates, garnish the kebabs with fresh coriander and serve immediately with pilau rice and warm naan bread.

> **Cook's Tip**
> For a special occasion or when cooking these kebabs on a barbecue, serve with a yogurt dip. Mix together 250ml/8fl oz/1 cup natural (plain) yogurt, 30ml/2 tbsp double (heavy) cream, 30ml/2 tbsp chopped fresh mint and ½ peeled, seeded and finely chopped cucumber in a bowl. Season to taste with salt and pepper. Cover with clear film (plastic wrap) and chill in the refrigerator until ready to serve. As an alternative to the mint you could use chopped fresh coriander (cilantro).

Chinese Chicken with Cashew Nuts

The cashew nuts give this dish a delightful crunchy texture that contrasts well with the noodles.

Serves 4

4 skinless chicken breast fillets
  (about 175g/6oz each)
3 garlic cloves, crushed
60ml/4 tbsp soy sauce
30ml/2 tbsp cornflour
  (cornstarch)
225g/8oz/4 cups dried
egg noodles
45ml/3 tbsp groundnut (peanut)
  or sunflower oil
15ml/1 tbsp sesame oil
115g/4oz/1 cup roasted
  cashew nuts
6 spring onions (scallions), cut
  into 5cm/2in pieces and
  halved lengthways
spring onion curls and a little
  chopped fresh red chilli,
  to garnish

1 Slice the chicken into strips, place in a bowl and stir in the garlic, soy sauce and cornflour. Cover with clear film (plastic wrap) and chill in the refrigerator for about 30 minutes.

2 Meanwhile, bring a pan of water to the boil and add the egg noodles. Turn off the heat and leave to stand for 5 minutes. Drain well and reserve.

3 Heat the oils in a large frying pan or wok. Add the chilled chicken and marinade juices and stir-fry over high heat for 3–4 minutes, or until golden brown.

4 Add the cashew nuts and spring onions to the pan or wok and stir-fry for a further 2–3 minutes.

5 Add the drained noodles and stir-fry for 2 minutes more. Toss the noodles well and serve immediately, garnished with the spring onion curls and chopped chilli.

> **Cook's Tip**
> For a milder garnish, seed the red chilli before chopping or finely dice some red (bell) pepper instead.

Tandoori Energy 222kcal/937kJ; Protein 42.8g; Carbohydrate 2g, of which sugars 1.7g; Fat 4.8g, of which saturates 0.9g; Cholesterol 123mg; Calcium 34mg; Fibre 0.2g; Sodium 115mg.
Chinese Energy 717kcal/3007kJ; Protein 55.5g; Carbohydrate 54.3g, of which sugars 4.2g; Fat 32.3g, of which saturates 6.1g; Cholesterol 139mg; Calcium 44mg; Fibre 2.8g; Sodium 1363mg.

Duck, Avocado & Berry Salad

In this Mediterranean dish, duck breasts are roasted with a honey and soy glaze until crisp, then served warm with fresh raspberries and avocado.

Serves 4
4 small or 2 large duck breast
  portions, halved if large
15ml/1 tbsp clear honey
15ml/1 tbsp dark soy sauce
mixed chopped fresh salad leaves
  such as lamb's lettuce or frisée
2 avocados, stoned (pitted),
  peeled and cut into chunks
115g/4oz/1 cup raspberries
salt and ground black pepper

For the dressing
60ml/4 tbsp olive oil
15ml/1 tbsp raspberry vinegar
15ml/1 tbsp redcurrant jelly

1 Preheat the oven to 220°C/425°F/Gas 7. Prick the skin of each duck breast portion with a fork. Blend the honey and soy sauce together in a small bowl, then brush the mixture all over the skins of the duck.

2 Place the duck breast portions on a rack set over a roasting pan and season with salt and pepper. Roast for 15–20 minutes, until the skins are crisp and the meat cooked.

3 Meanwhile, to make the dressing, put the oil, vinegar and redcurrant jelly in a small bowl, season with salt and pepper and whisk well until evenly blended.

4 Slice the duck breast portions diagonally and arrange on four individual plates with the salad leaves, avocados and raspberries. Spoon the dressing over the top and serve immediately.

> **Cook's Tip**
> *Small avocados contain the most flavour and have a good texture. They should be ripe but not too soft, so avoid any with skins that are turning black.*

Chinese-style Chicken Salad

For a variation and to add more colour, add some cooked, peeled prawns to this lovely salad.

Serves 4
4 chicken breast fillets (about
  175g/6oz each)
60ml/4 tbsp dark soy sauce
pinch of Chinese five-spice powder
squeeze of lemon juice
1/2 cucumber, peeled and cut into
  thin batons
5ml/1 tsp salt
45ml/3 tbsp sunflower oil
30ml/2 tbsp sesame oil
15ml/1 tbsp sesame seeds
30ml/2 tbsp Chinese rice wine or
  dry sherry
2 carrots, cut into thin batons
8 spring onions
  (scallions), shredded
75g/3oz/1 cup beansprouts

For the sauce
60ml/4 tbsp crunchy
  peanut butter
10ml/2 tsp lemon juice
10ml/2 tsp sesame oil
1.5ml/1/4 tsp hot chilli powder
1 spring onion, finely chopped

1 Put the chicken into a pan and pour in water to cover. Add 15ml/1 tbsp of the soy sauce, the Chinese five-spice powder and lemon juice. Cover and bring to the boil, then lower the heat and simmer for 20 minutes. Drain the chicken and remove and discard the skin. Slice the flesh into thin strips.

2 Sprinkle the cucumber batons with salt, leave for 30 minutes, then rinse well and pat dry with kitchen paper.

3 Heat the oils in a small frying pan. Add the sesame seeds and cook for 30 seconds, then stir in the remaining soy sauce and the rice wine or sherry. Add the carrot batons and stir-fry for 2 minutes, then remove the pan from the heat.

4 Mix together the cucumber, spring onions, beansprouts, carrots, pan juices and chicken. Transfer to a shallow dish. Cover with clear film (plastic wrap) and chill in the refrigerator for 1 hour.

5 For the sauce, cream the first four ingredients together, then stir in the spring onion. Serve the chicken with the sauce.

Chicken Energy 452kcal/1886kJ; Protein 47g; Carbohydrate 4.1g, of which sugars 3g; Fat 27.2g, of which saturates 4.8g; Cholesterol 123mg; Calcium 53mg; Fibre 1.5g; Sodium 1720mg.
Duck Energy 345kcal/1438kJ; Protein 21.2g; Carbohydrate 8g, of which sugars 7.3g; Fat 27.2g, of which saturates 5g; Cholesterol 110mg; Calcium 26mg; Fibre 2.4g; Sodium 382mg.

Crumbed Turkey Steaks

The authentic Austrian dish, *wiener schnitzel*, uses veal escalopes, but turkey steaks make a tasty alternative.

Serves 4

4 turkey breast steaks (about 150g/5oz each)
40g/1½oz/⅓ cup plain (all-purpose) flour, seasoned
1 egg, lightly beaten
75g/3oz/1½ cups fresh white breadcrumbs
75ml/5 tbsp finely grated Parmesan cheese
25g/1oz/2 tbsp butter
45ml/3 tbsp sunflower oil
fresh parsley sprigs, to garnish
4 lemon wedges, to serve

1 Lay the turkey steaks between two sheets of clear film (plastic wrap). Beat each one with a rolling pin until flattened and even. Snip the edges of the steaks with kitchen scissors a few times to prevent them from curling during cooking.

2 Place the seasoned flour on one plate, the egg in a shallow bowl and the breadcrumbs and Parmesan mixed together on another plate.

3 Dip each side of the steaks into the flour and shake off any excess. Next, dip them into the egg and then gently press each side into the breadcrumbs and cheese until evenly coated.

4 Heat the butter and oil in a large frying pan over medium heat. Add the turkey steaks and cook for 2–3 minutes on each side, until golden. Transfer to warmed plates, garnish with fresh parsley sprigs and serve with lemon wedges.

Cook's Tip
The easiest way to make breadcrumbs is in a food processor. Tear the bread into 2.5cm/1in pieces and process in brief bursts with a metal blade. You can also use a blender in the same way, but work in small batches, emptying each one into a bowl before adding more bread. The traditional way is, of course, to use a grater, taking care not to damage your fingers.

Country Cider Hot-pot

Rabbit meat is now beginning to regain its popularity – it never lost it in some European countries – and, like all game, is a healthy, low-fat option.

Serves 4

25g/1oz/¼ cup plain (all-purpose) flour
4 boneless rabbit portions
25g/1oz/2 tbsp butter
15ml/1 tbsp vegetable oil
15 baby (pearl) onions
4 rashers (strips) streaky (fatty) bacon, chopped
10ml/2 tsp Dijon mustard
450ml/¾ pint/1¾ cups dry (hard) cider
3 carrots, chopped
2 parsnips, chopped
12 ready-to-eat prunes
1 fresh rosemary sprig
1 bay leaf
salt and ground black pepper
mashed potatoes, to serve (optional)

1 Preheat the oven to 160°C/325°F/Gas 3. Place the flour in a plastic bag, season with salt and pepper and shake to mix. Add the rabbit portions and shake until coated. Remove from the bag and set aside.

2 Heat the butter and oil in a flameproof casserole over medium-low heat. Add the onions and bacon and cook, stirring occasionally, for about 4 minutes, until the onions have softened. Remove with a slotted spoon and set aside.

3 Add the rabbit portions to the casserole and cook, turning frequently, for 8–10 minutes, until evenly browned all over. Spread a little of the mustard over the top of each portion.

4 Return the onions and bacon to the casserole, pour in the cider and add the carrots, parsnips, prunes, rosemary and bay leaf. Season generously with salt and pepper. Bring to the boil, then cover with a tight-fitting lid and transfer to the oven. Cook for about 1½ hours, until the meat is cooked through and the vegetables are tender.

5 Remove and discard the rosemary sprig and bay leaf and serve the rabbit hot with creamy mashed potatoes, if you like.

Turkey Energy 565kcal/2376kJ; Protein 64.9g; Carbohydrate 24.3g, of which sugars 0.7g; Fat 24g, of which saturates 9.4g; Cholesterol 191mg; Calcium 283mg; Fibre 0.8g; Sodium 538mg.
Hot-pot Energy 544kcal/2279kJ; Protein 41.1g; Carbohydrate 42.9g, of which sugars 32.2g; Fat 21g, of which saturates 8.2g; Cholesterol 136mg; Calcium 129mg; Fibre 8g; Sodium 488mg.

Turkey Pastitsio

A traditional Greek *pastitsio* is a rich, high-fat dish made with beef, but this lighter version is just as tasty.

Serves 4–6

450g/1lb lean minced (ground) turkey
1 large onion, finely chopped
60ml/4 tbsp tomato purée (paste)
250ml/8fl oz/1 cup red wine or chicken stock
5ml/1 tsp ground cinnamon
300g/11oz/3 cups macaroni
300ml/½ pint/1¼ cups skimmed milk
25g/1oz/2 tbsp sunflower margarine
25g/1oz/¼ cup plain (all-purpose) flour
5ml/1 tsp grated nutmeg
2 tomatoes, sliced
60ml/4 tbsp wholemeal (whole-wheat) breadcrumbs
salt and ground black pepper
green salad, to serve

1 Preheat the oven to 220°C/425°F/Gas 7. Fry the turkey and onion in a non-stick frying pan without adding any fat, stirring until the turkey is lightly browned.

2 Stir in the tomato purée, red wine or stock and cinnamon. Season with salt and pepper, then cover with a tight-fitting lid and simmer for 5 minutes.

3 Bring a pan of salted water to the boil, add the macaroni, bring back to the boil and cook for 8–10 minutes, until just tender. Drain well.

4 Spoon alternate layers of macaroni and the meat mixture into a wide ovenproof dish.

5 Place the milk, margarine and flour in a pan and whisk over medium heat until thickened and smooth. Add the nutmeg and season with salt and pepper to taste.

6 Pour the sauce evenly over the pasta and meat. Arrange the tomato slices on top and sprinkle lines of breadcrumbs over the surface. Bake for 30–35 minutes, or until golden brown and bubbling. Serve hot with a green salad.

Tuscan Chicken

A simple peasant casserole with all the flavours of Tuscan ingredients. The white wine can be replaced by chicken stock.

Serves 4

5ml/1 tsp olive oil
8 chicken thighs, skinned
1 onion, thinly sliced
2 red (bell) peppers, seeded and sliced
1 garlic clove, crushed
300ml/½ pint/1¼ cups passata (bottled strained tomatoes)
150ml/¼ pint/½ cup dry white wine
large fresh oregano sprig, or 5ml/1 tsp dried oregano
400g/14oz can cannellini beans, drained and rinsed
45ml/3 tbsp fresh breadcrumbs
salt and ground black pepper
fresh oregano or flat leaf parsley sprigs, to garnish

1 Heat the oil in a large, heavy pan over medium heat. Add the chicken and cook, turning frequently, for 8–10 minutes, until golden brown all over. Remove the chicken from the pan and keep hot.

2 Add the onion and red peppers to the pan, lower the heat and cook, stirring occasionally, for about 5 minutes, until softened but not coloured. Stir in the garlic.

3 Return the chicken to the pan and add the passata, wine and oregano. Season well with salt and pepper, bring to the boil, then cover the pan with a tight-fitting lid.

4 Lower the heat and simmer gently, stirring occasionally, for 30–35 minutes, or until the chicken is tender and the juices run clear when the thickest par is pierced with the point of a knife.

5 Preheat the grill (broiler). Stir in the cannellini beans and simmer for a further 5 minutes until heated through. Sprinkle with the breadcrumbs and cook under the grill for a few minutes, until golden brown.

6 Divide the chicken, beans and vegetables among warmed serving plates, garnish with herb sprigs and serve immediately.

Turkey Energy 406kcal/1716kJ; Protein 28.9g; Carbohydrate 56.8g, of which sugars 9.5g; Fat 5.5g, of which saturates 0.4g; Cholesterol 45mg; Calcium 117mg; Fibre 3.1g; Sodium 202mg.
Chicken Energy 379kcal/1599kJ; Protein 41.3g; Carbohydrate 35.8g, of which sugars 12.6g; Fat 6.2g, of which saturates 1.5g; Cholesterol 158mg; Calcium 118mg; Fibre 8.5g; Sodium 789mg.

Minty Yogurt Chicken

Marinated, grilled chicken thighs make a tasty light lunch or supper – and they are an economical buy, too.

Serves 4

8 chicken thigh portions

15ml/1 tbsp clear honey
30ml/2 tbsp lime juice
30ml/2 tbsp natural (plain) yogurt
60ml/4 tbsp chopped fresh mint
salt and ground black pepper
boiled new potatoes and tomato
 salad, to serve (optional)

1 Skin the chicken thighs and slash the flesh at intervals with a sharp knife. Place them in a non-metal bowl. Mix together the honey, lime juice, yogurt and half the mint in another bowl and season with salt and pepper.

2 Spoon the marinade over the chicken, cover the bowl with clear film (plastic wrap) and leave to marinate in a cool place for 30 minutes.

3 Line a grill (broiler) pan with foil and preheat the grill (broiler). Remove the chicken from the marinade, place in the pan and cook, turning occasionally, for 15–20 minutes, until golden brown and the juices run clear when thickest part is pierced with point of a sharp knife.

4 Transfer the chicken thighs to warmed plates, sprinkle with the remaining mint and serve immediately with potatoes and tomato salad, if you like.

Cook's Tip
If you want to marinate the chicken for longer than 30 minutes, place the bowl in the refrigerator.

Variation
Substitute chicken drumsticks for the thighs and increase the cooking time by 5–10 minutes.

Mandarin Sesame Duck

The rind, juice and flesh of sweet mandarin oranges are used in this delightful dish.

Serves 4

4 duck leg or breast fillets
30ml/2 tbsp light soy sauce

45ml/3 tbsp clear honey
15ml/1 tbsp sesame seeds
4 mandarin oranges
5ml/1 tsp cornflour (cornstarch)
salt and ground black pepper

1 Preheat the oven to 180°C/350°F/Gas 4. Prick the duck skin all over. Slash the breast skin diagonally at intervals. Roast the duck for 1 hour. Mix 15ml/1 tbsp soy sauce with 30ml/2 tbsp honey and brush over the duck. Sprinkle with sesame seeds. Roast for a further 15 minutes.

2 Grate the rind from one mandarin and squeeze the juice from two. Place in a small pan and stir in the cornflour, remaining soy sauce and honey. Heat, stirring, until thickened and clear. Season with salt and pepper. Peel and slice the remaining mandarins. Serve the duck with the mandarin slices and sauce.

Sticky Ginger Chicken

For a fuller flavour, marinate the chicken drumsticks in the glaze for 30 minutes.

Serves 4

8 chicken drumsticks

30ml/2 tbsp lemon juice
25g/1oz light muscovado
 (brown) sugar
5ml/1 tsp grated fresh root ginger
10ml/2 tsp soy sauce
ground black pepper

1 Slash the chicken drumsticks about three times through the thickest part of the flesh. Mix all the remaining ingredients in a bowl, then toss the drumsticks in the glaze.

2 Cook them under a hot grill (broiler) or on a barbecue, turning occasionally and brushing with the glaze, until golden and the juices run clear when the thickest part is pierced.

Minty Yogurt Energy 179kcal/752kJ; Protein 31.8g; Carbohydrate 3.4g, of which sugars 3.4g; Fat 4.3g, of which saturates 1.3g; Cholesterol 158mg; Calcium 25mg; Fibre 0g; Sodium 142mg.
Mandarin Duck Energy 254kcal/1066kJ; Protein 31g; Carbohydrate 12g, of which sugars 10.9g; Fat 12g, of which saturates 2.3g; Cholesterol 165mg; Calcium 55mg; Fibre 0.5g; Sodium 704mg.
Sticky Ginger Energy 234kcal/980kJ; Protein 29.2g; Carbohydrate 6.5g, of which sugars 6.5g; Fat 10.3g, of which saturates 2.7g; Cholesterol 155mg; Calcium 20mg; Fibre 0g; Sodium 145mg.

Oat-crusted Chicken with Sage

Oats make an excellent, crunchy coating for savoury foods, and offer a good way to add extra fibre.

Serves 4

45ml/3 tbsp milk
10ml/2 tsp English (hot) mustard
40g/1½oz/½ cup rolled oats
45ml/3 tbsp chopped fresh
  sage leaves
8 chicken thighs or
  drumsticks, skinned
120ml/4fl oz/½ cup fromage
  frais (farmer's cheese)
5ml/1 tsp wholegrain mustard
salt and ground black pepper
fresh sage leaves, to garnish

1 Preheat the oven to 200°C/400°F/Gas 6. Mix together the milk and mustard in a small bowl.

2 Mix the oats with 30ml/2 tbsp of the chopped sage on a plate and season with salt and pepper. Brush the chicken with the milk mixture and press into the oats to coat evenly.

3 Place the chicken on a baking sheet and bake for about 40 minutes, or until the juices run clear when the thickest part is pierced with the point of a sharp knife.

4 Meanwhile, mix together the fromage frais, wholegrain mustard and remaining sage in a bowl and season to taste with salt and pepper. Transfer to a small serving dish.

5 Place the chicken on warmed serving plates and garnish with fresh sage leaves. Serve immediately with the dish of sauce.

> **Cook's Tips**
> • If fresh sage is not available, choose another fresh herb, such as thyme, parsley or tarragon. Sage is one of those herbs that does not dry well, quickly becoming dusty and flavourless.
> • These chicken thighs or drumsticks may be served hot or cold. They would be a good choice for a picnic. Pack the sauce separately in a plastic container or screw-top jar.
> • If you find English (hot) mustard too spicy, substitute Dijon.

Chicken in Creamy Orange Sauce

The brandy adds a rich flavour to this French dish, but omit it if you prefer and use orange juice alone.

Serves 4

8 chicken thighs or
  drumsticks, skinned
45ml/3 tbsp brandy
300ml/½ pint/1¼ cups fresh
  orange juice
3 spring onions
  (scallions), chopped
10ml/2 tsp cornflour (cornstarch)
90ml/6 tbsp fromage frais
  (farmer's cheese)
salt and ground black pepper
boiled rice or pasta and green
  salad, to serve (optional)

1 Cook the chicken pieces in a non-stick or heavy frying pan, without any added fat, over medium-low heat for 8–10 minutes, turning frequently until evenly browned all over.

2 Stir in the brandy, orange juice and spring onions and bring to the boil. Lower the heat, cover and simmer gently for about 15 minutes, or until the chicken is tender and the juices run clear when the thickest part is pierced with the point of a sharp knife.

3 Blend the cornflour with a little water in a small bowl, then mix into the fromage frais. Stir this into a small pan and cook over medium heat until boiling.

4 Season the sauce to taste with salt and pepper. Spoon the chicken and cooking juices on to warmed plates, pour the sauce over it and serve with plain boiled rice or pasta and green salad, if you like.

> **Cook's Tip**
> For an even healthier version of this dish, suitable for those who are watching their weight or cholesterol levels, use low-fat fromage frais (farmer's cheese) which is virtually fat-free. The sauce will still be beautifully creamy and rich tasting.

Oat-crusted Energy 238kcal/997kJ; Protein 32.2g; Carbohydrate 3g, of which sugars 3g; Fat 10.9g, of which saturates 3.1g; Cholesterol 157mg; Calcium 66mg; Fibre 0g; Sodium 163mg.
In Orange Sauce Energy 306kcal/1287kJ; Protein 43.7g; Carbohydrate 10.1g, of which sugars 7.7g; Fat 7.5g, of which saturates 2.9g; Cholesterol 212mg; Calcium 50mg; Fibre 0.2g; Sodium 198mg.

Duck with Orange Sauce

This is a simple, yet more elegant-looking variation on the classic French whole duck.

Serves 4
4 duck breast portions
15ml/1 tbsp sunflower oil
2 oranges

150ml/¼ pint/⅔ cup fresh
    orange juice
15ml/1 tbsp port
30ml/2 tbsp Seville (Temple)
    orange marmalade
15g/½oz/1 tbsp butter
5ml/1 tsp cornflour (cornstarch)
salt and ground black pepper

1 Season the duck skin with salt and pepper. Heat the oil in a frying pan over a medium heat. Add the duck breast portions, skin-side down, cover and cook for 3–4 minutes, until just lightly browned. Turn the duck over, lower the heat slightly and cook, uncovered, for 5–6 minutes.

2 Peel the skin from the oranges and remove the white pith. Working over a bowl to catch any juice, slice either side of the membranes with a sharp knife to release the orange segments. Set the segments aside with the juice.

3 Remove the duck portions from the pan with a slotted spoon, drain on kitchen paper and keep warm in the oven while making the sauce.

4 Drain off the fat from the frying pan. Add the segmented oranges, all but 30ml/2 tbsp of the orange juice, the port and the orange marmalade. Bring to the boil and then reduce the heat slightly. Gradually whisk small knobs (pats) of the butter into the sauce, one piece at a time, and season to taste with salt and pepper.

5 Blend the cornflour with the reserved orange juice in a small bowl, pour into the pan and stir until the sauce has thickened slightly. Return the duck to the pan and cook over low heat for about 3 minutes. Remove the duck portions from the pan and cut into thick slices. Arrange them on warmed plates and spoon the sauce over them. Serve immediately.

Normandy Roast Chicken

The chicken is turned over halfway through roasting so that it cooks evenly and stays wonderfully moist.

Serves 4
50g/2oz/¼ cup butter, softened
30ml/2 tbsp chopped
    fresh tarragon

1 small garlic clove, crushed
1.5kg/3–3½lb fresh chicken
5ml/1 tsp plain (all-purpose) flour
150ml/¼ pint/⅔ cup double
    (heavy) cream
squeeze of lemon juice
salt and ground black pepper
fresh tarragon and lemon slices,
    to garnish

1 Preheat the oven to 200°C/400°F/Gas 6. Mix together the butter, 15ml/1 tbsp of the chopped tarragon and the garlic in a bowl and season with salt and pepper. Spoon half the butter mixture into the cavity of the chicken.

2 Carefully lift the skin at the neck end of the bird from the breast flesh on each side, then gently push a little of the butter mixture into each pocket and smooth it down over the breasts with your fingers.

3 Season the bird and lay it, breast-side down, in a roasting pan. Roast for 45 minutes, then turn the chicken over and baste with the cooking juices. Cook for a further 45 minutes, until the juices run clear when the thickest part of the chicken is pierced with the point of a sharp knife.

4 When the chicken is cooked, lift it to drain out any juices from the cavity into the pan, then transfer the bird to a warmed platter, cover and keep warm.

5 Place the roasting pan over low heat and heat until sizzling. Stir in the flour and cook, stirring constantly, for 1 minute, then stir in the cream, the remaining tarragon, 150ml/¼ pint/⅔ cup water and the lemon juice. Season to taste with salt and pepper. Bring to the boil and cook, stirring constantly, for 2–3 minutes, until thickened. Carve the chicken into slices and place them on warmed plates. Garnish with tarragon and lemon slices and serve with the sauce handed separately.

Roast Chicken Energy 491kcal/2038kJ; Protein 37.6g; Carbohydrate 1.2g, of which sugars 1.1g; Fat 37.3g, of which saturates 17.8g; Cholesterol 210mg; Calcium 71mg; Fibre 0.5g; Sodium 228mg.
Duck Breasts Energy 307kcal/1289kJ; Protein 30.6g; Carbohydrate 16.5g, of which sugars 15.4g; Fat 15.7g, of which saturates 4.2g; Cholesterol 173mg; Calcium 60mg; Fibre 1.3g; Sodium 201mg.

Pot-roast Poussin

This dish is inspired by the French method of cooking these birds. Pot-roasting keeps them beautifully moist and succulent.

Serves 4

15ml/1 tbsp olive oil
1 onion, sliced
1 large garlic clove, sliced
50g/2oz/⅓ cup diced
  smoked bacon
2 poussins (about 450g/
  1lb each)
30ml/2 tbsp melted butter
2 baby celery hearts, each cut
  into 4 pieces

8 baby carrots
2 small courgettes (zucchini), cut
  into chunks
8 small new potatoes
600ml/1 pint/2½ cups chicken
  stock
150ml/¼ pint/⅔ cup dry
  white wine
1 bay leaf
2 fresh thyme sprigs
2 fresh rosemary sprigs
15ml/1 tbsp butter, softened
15g/½oz/2 tbsp plain (all-
  purpose) flour
salt and ground black pepper
fresh herbs, to garnish

1 Preheat the oven to 190°C/375°F/Gas 5. Heat the olive oil in a large flameproof casserole over low heat. Add the onions, garlic and bacon and cook, stirring occasionally, for 5–6 minutes, until the onions have softened. Brush the poussins with half the melted butter and season with salt and pepper. Add to the casserole with the vegetables. Pour in the stock and wine and add the herbs. Cover and bake for 20 minutes.

2 Remove the lid and brush the birds with the remaining melted butter. Bake for a further 25–30 minutes, until golden. Transfer the poussins to a warmed serving platter and cut each in half with poultry shears or scissors. Remove the vegetables with a slotted spoon and arrange them around the birds. Cover with foil and keep warm.

3 Remove the herbs from the casserole and discard. Mix the butter and flour to a paste. Bring the cooking liquid to the boil, then whisk in spoonfuls of paste until thickened. Season with salt and pepper and serve with the poussins and vegetables, garnished with herbs.

Coq au Vin

Chicken is flamed in brandy, then braised in red wine with bacon, mushrooms and onions in this classic dish.

Serves 4

50g/2oz/½ cup plain
  (all-purpose) flour
1.5kg/3–3½ lb chicken, cut into
  8 pieces
15ml/1 tbsp olive oil
65g/2½oz/5 tbsp butter
20 baby (pearl) onions

75g/3oz/½ cup diced streaky
  (fatty) bacon
about 20 button
  (white) mushrooms
30ml/2 tbsp brandy
1 bottle red Burgundy wine
bouquet garni
3 garlic cloves
5ml/1 tsp soft light brown sugar
salt and ground black pepper
15ml/1 tbsp chopped fresh
  parsley and croûtons, to garnish

1 Place 40g/1½oz/⅓ cup of the flour in a large plastic bag, season with salt and pepper and add the chicken pieces. Shake well to coat. Heat the oil and 50g/2oz/4 tbsp of the butter in a large flameproof casserole over low heat. Add the onions and bacon and cook, stirring occasionally, for about 10 minutes, until the onions have browned lightly. Add the mushrooms and cook for 2 minutes more. Remove with a slotted spoon and reserve.

2 Add the chicken pieces to the casserole, increase the heat to medium and cook, turning frequently, for about 5–6 minutes, until evenly browned all over. Add the brandy and, standing well back, ignite it with a match, then shake the casserole gently until the flames subside.

3 Add the wine, bouquet garni, garlic and sugar and season with salt and pepper. Bring to the boil, lower the heat, cover and simmer, stirring occasionally, for 1 hour. Add the onions, bacon and mushrooms, re-cover and cook for 30 minutes. Transfer the chicken, vegetables and bacon to a warmed dish.

4 Remove the bouquet garni and boil the liquid for 2 minutes. Cream the remaining butter and flour. Whisk in spoonfuls of the mixture to thicken the liquid. Pour the sauce over the chicken and serve garnished with parsley and croûtons.

Poussin Energy 549kcal/2290kJ; Protein 30.8g; Carbohydrate 25.8g, of which sugars 7.5g; Fat 34g, of which saturates 12.4g; Cholesterol 163mg; Calcium 76mg; Fibre 3.5g; Sodium 372mg.
Coq au Vin Energy 630kcal/2618kJ; Protein 42.8g; Carbohydrate 19.3g, of which sugars 7.4g; Fat 41g, of which saturates 17.3g; Cholesterol 209mg; Calcium 67mg; Fibre 2.6g; Sodium 480mg.

Moroccan Spiced Roast Poussin

The poussins are stuffed with a fruity and aromatic rice mixture and glazed with spiced yogurt in this flavoursome dish. One bird is sufficient for two servings.

Serves 4
75g/3oz/1 cup cooked long
    grain rice
1 small onion, chopped
finely grated rind and juice of
    1 lemon
30ml/2 tbsp chopped fresh mint
45ml/3 tbsp chopped
    dried apricots
30ml/2 tbsp natural
    (plain) yogurt
10ml/2 tsp ground turmeric
10ml/2 tsp ground cumin
2 poussins (about 450g/1lb each)
salt and ground black pepper
lemon slices and fresh mint
    sprigs, to garnish

1 Preheat the oven to 200°C/400°F/Gas 6. Mix together the rice, onion, lemon rind, mint and apricots in a bowl. Stir in half the lemon juice, half the yogurt, half the turmeric and half the cumin and season with salt and pepper.

2 Stuff the poussins with the rice mixture at the neck end only, taking care not to overfill them. Reserve the spare stuffing to be served separately. Place the poussins side by side on a rack in a roasting pan.

3 Mix together the remaining lemon juice, yogurt, turmeric and cumin in a small bowl, then brush this all over the poussins. Cover them loosely with foil and cook in the oven for 30 minutes.

4 Remove the foil and roast for a further 15 minutes, or until the poussins are golden brown and the juices run clear, when the thickest part is pierced with the point of a sharp knife.

5 Transfer both the poussins to a chopping board and cut them in half with a sharp knife or poultry shears. Place half a bird on each of four warmed plates. Garnish with slices of lemon and fresh mint sprigs and serve immediately with the remaining rice and apricot mixture.

Chilli Chicken Couscous

Couscous is a very easy alternative to rice and makes a good base for all kinds of ingredients.

Serves 4
225g/8oz/2 cups couscous
1 litre/1¼ pints/4 cups boiling
    water
5ml/1 tsp olive oil
400g/14oz skinless boneless
    chicken, diced
1 yellow (bell) pepper, seeded
    and sliced
2 large courgettes (zucchini),
    thickly sliced
1 small green chilli, thinly sliced, or
    5ml/1 tsp chilli sauce
1 large tomato, diced
425g/15oz can chickpeas,
    drained and rinsed
salt and ground black pepper
fresh coriander (cilantro) or
    parsley sprigs, to garnish

1 Place the couscous in a large bowl and pour the boiling water over it. Cover and leave to stand for 30 minutes.

2 Heat the oil in a large, non-stick frying pan over medium heat. Add the chicken and stir-fry quickly to seal, then reduce the heat to low.

3 Stir in the yellow pepper, courgettes and chilli or chilli sauce and cook, stirring occasionally, for about 10 minutes, until the vegetables are softened.

4 Stir in the tomato and chickpeas, then add the couscous. Season to taste with salt and pepper and cook over medium heat, stirring constantly, until hot. Serve immediately garnished with sprigs of fresh coriander or parsley.

Cook's Tip
You can use dried chickpeas in this recipe. Soak them overnight in cold water, then drain, place in a pan and add water to cover. Bring to the boil, then cook for 2–2½ hours, until tender. Drain well and add to the pan in step 4. Some cooks like to add a pinch of bicarbonate of soda (baking soda) to the water when cooking chickpeas, but this is not essential.

Poussin Energy 354kcal/1478kJ; Protein 27g; Carbohydrate 20.3g, of which sugars 5g; Fat 18.4g, of which saturates 5g; Cholesterol 131mg; Calcium 25mg; Fibre 0.9g; Sodium 92mg.
Chicken Energy 394kcal/1661kJ; Protein 36.8g; Carbohydrate 50.9g, of which sugars 5.2g; Fat 6.1g, of which saturates 0.9g; Cholesterol 70mg; Calcium 86mg; Fibre 6g; Sodium 299mg.

Mediterranean Turkey Skewers

These skewers are easy to
assemble, and can be
cooked under a grill or on a
charcoal barbecue.

Serves 4
90ml/6 tbsp olive oil
45ml/3 tbsp lemon juice
1 garlic clove, finely chopped
30ml/2 tbsp chopped fresh basil

2 courgettes (zucchini)
1 long thin aubergine (eggplant)
300g/11oz skinless boneless
   turkey, cut into 5cm/2in cubes
12–16 baby onions
1 red or yellow (bell) pepper,
   seeded and cut into 5cm/
   2in squares
salt and ground black pepper

1 Mix the olive oil with the lemon juice, garlic and basil in a
small bowl. Season with salt and pepper.

2 Slice the courgettes and aubergine lengthways into strips
5mm/¼in thick. Cut the strips crossways about two-thirds of
the way along their length. Discard the shorter lengths. Wrap
half the turkey pieces with the courgette slices and the other
half with the aubergine slices.

3 Prepare the skewers by alternating the turkey, onions and
pepper pieces. (If you are using wooden skewers, soak them in
water first. This will prevent them from charring during
cooking.) Lay the prepared skewers on a platter and sprinkle
with the flavoured oil. Cover with clear film (plastic wrap) and
leave to marinate in a cool place for at least 30 minutes.
Preheat the grill (broiler).

4 Grill (broil), turning occasionally, for 10 minutes, until the
vegetables are tender and the turkey is cooked through.
Transfer the skewers to warmed plates and serve immediately.

Variation
*For extra colour, substitute red and yellow cherry tomatoes
for the pickled onions or simply add one tomato to each end of
each skewer.*

Duck with Chestnut Sauce

Chestnuts play an important
role in Italian cooking. This
autumnal dish makes use of
the sweet chestnuts that
are freely gathered in the
woods there.

Serves 4–5
1 fresh rosemary sprig
1 garlic clove, sliced
30ml/2 tbsp olive oil
4 duck breast fillets, trimmed of
   visible fat

For the sauce
450g/1lb/4 cups chestnuts
5ml/1 tsp olive oil
350ml/12fl oz/1½ cups milk
1 small onion, finely chopped
1 carrot, finely chopped
1 small bay leaf
30ml/2 tbsp cream, warmed
salt and ground black pepper

1 Pull the needles from the sprig of rosemary. Combine them
with the garlic and oil in a shallow bowl. Pat the duck breast
fillets dry with kitchen paper. Brush them with the marinade
and leave to stand for at least 2 hours before cooking.

2 Preheat the oven to 180°C/350°F/Gas 4. Cut a cross in the
flat side of each chestnut with a sharp knife. Place the chestnuts
on a baking sheet with the oil and shake the sheet until they are
coated. Bake for 20 minutes, then remove from the oven and
peel when they are cool enough to handle.

3 Place the chestnuts in a heavy pan with the milk, onion, carrot
and bay leaf. Cook over low heat for 10–15 minutes, until the
chestnuts are tender, then season with salt and pepper. Discard
the bay leaf. Press the mixture through a sieve (strainer).

4 Return the sauce to the pan. Heat gently while the duck
breasts are cooking. Just before serving, stir in the cream. If the
sauce is too thick, add a little more cream. Preheat the grill
(broiler) or prepare a barbecue.

5 Cook the duck breasts until medium-rare, for 6–8 minutes.
They should be pink inside. Slice into rounds and arrange on
warmed plates. Serve with the heated sauce.

Turkey Energy 315kcal/1311kJ; Protein 22.7g; Carbohydrate 16.1g, of which sugars 12.9g; Fat 18.2g, of which saturates 2.8g; Cholesterol 43mg; Calcium 70mg; Fibre 4.9g; Sodium 46mg.
Duck Energy 366kcal/1535kJ; Protein 25.9g; Carbohydrate 35.2g, of which sugars 8.2g; Fat 16.4g, of which saturates 3.5g; Cholesterol 135mg; Calcium 68mg; Fibre 4.2g; Sodium 148mg.

Chicken Tikka

The red food colourings give this dish its traditional bright colour. Serve with lemon wedges and a crisp mixed salad.

Serves 4

1.75kg/3½lb chicken
mixed fresh salad leaves such as frisée, oakleaf lettuce or radicchio, and lemon wedges to serve

For the marinade

150ml/¼ pint/⅔ cup natural (plain) yogurt
5ml/1 tsp ground paprika
10ml/2 tsp grated fresh root ginger
1 garlic clove, crushed
10ml/2 tsp garam masala
2.5ml/½ tsp salt
red food colouring (optional)
juice of 1 lemon

1 Cut the chicken into eight even-size pieces, using a sharp knife or cleaver.

2 Mix all the marinade ingredients in a large dish, add the chicken pieces and turn to coat. Cover with clear film (plastic wrap) and leave in the refrigerator for 4 hours or overnight to allow the flavours to penetrate the flesh.

3 Preheat the oven to 200°C/400°F/Gas 6. Remove the chicken pieces from the marinade and arrange them in a single layer in a large ovenproof dish. Reserve the marinade. Bake the chicken, basting occasionally with the marinade, for 30–40 minutes, or until tender.

4 Arrange on a bed of salad leaves on individual plates, top with the chicken and serve immediately with lemon wedges. Alternatively, leave the chicken to cool, then serve cold on a bed of salad leaves.

Cook's Tip

This dish would also make an excellent appetizer. Cut the chicken into smaller pieces and reduce the cooking time slightly, then serve with lemon wedges and a simple salad garnish.

Simple Chicken Curry

Curry powder can be bought in three different strengths – mild, medium and hot. Use whichever type you prefer.

Serves 4

8 chicken legs, each piece including thigh and drumstick
30ml/2 tbsp groundnut (peanut) oil
1 onion, thinly sliced
1 garlic clove, crushed
15ml/1 tbsp medium curry powder
25g/1oz/¼ cup plain (all-purpose) flour
450ml/¾ pint/scant 2 cups chicken stock
1 beefsteak tomato
15ml/1 tbsp mango chutney
15ml/1 tbsp lemon juice
salt and ground black pepper
boiled rice, to serve

1 Cut the chicken legs in half. Heat the oil in a large flameproof casserole over medium heat. Add the chicken pieces and cook, turning frequently, for 8–10 minutes, until evenly browned on both sides. Remove the chicken from the casserole and keep warm.

2 Add the onion and garlic to the casserole, lower the heat and cook, stirring occasionally, for about 5 minutes, until the onion is softened but not coloured. Stir in the curry powder and cook, stirring constantly, for a further 2 minutes.

3 Stir in the flour and cook, stirring constantly, for 1 minute, then gradually blend in the chicken stock, stirring well. Season with salt and pepper.

4 Bring to the boil, return the chicken pieces to the casserole, cover and simmer for 20–30 minutes, until tender.

5 Skin the beefsteak tomato by blanching in boiling water for about 15 seconds, then running it under cold water to loosen the skin. Peel and cut into small dice.

6 Add to the chicken with the mango chutney and lemon juice. Heat through gently and adjust the seasoning to taste. Serve with boiled rice and Indian accompaniments.

Tikka Energy 416kcal/1730kJ; Protein 46g; Carbohydrate 2.1g, of which sugars 0.2g; Fat 24.8g, of which saturates 8.5g; Cholesterol 203mg; Calcium 21mg; Fibre 0.5g; Sodium 173mg.
Curry Energy 571kcal/2392kJ; Protein 38.9g; Carbohydrate 78.9g, of which sugars 4g; Fat 10.8g, of which saturates 2g; Cholesterol 158mg; Calcium 43mg; Fibre 0.8g; Sodium 180mg.

Chicken Biryani

A biryani – from the Urdu – is a dish mixed with rice which resembles a risotto. It provides a one-pan meal.

Serves 4

275g/10oz/1½ cups basmati
    rice, rinsed and drained
2.5ml/½ tsp salt
5 cardamom pods
2–3 cloves
1 cinnamon stick
45ml/3 tbsp vegetable oil
3 onions, sliced
675g/1½lb skinless boneless
    chicken, diced
1.5ml/¼ tsp ground cloves
5 cardamom pods, seeds removed
    and ground
1.5ml/¼ tsp hot chilli powder

5ml/1 tsp ground cumin
5ml/1 tsp ground coriander
2.5ml/½ tsp ground black pepper
3 garlic cloves, finely chopped
5ml/1 tsp finely chopped fresh
    root ginger
juice of 1 lemon
4 tomatoes, sliced
30ml/2 tbsp chopped fresh
    coriander (cilantro)
150ml/¼ pint/⅔ cup natural
    (plain) yogurt
2.5ml/½ tsp saffron threads
    soaked in 10ml/2 tsp hot milk
45ml/3 tbsp toasted flaked
    (sliced) almonds and fresh
    coriander sprigs, to garnish
natural yogurt, to serve

1 Preheat the oven to 190°C/375°F/Gas 5. Bring a large pan of salted water to the boil and add the rice, salt, cardamom pods, cloves and cinnamon stick. Bring back to the boil and cook for 2 minutes. Drain, leaving the whole spices in the rice.

2 Heat the oil in a frying pan over low heat. Add the onions and cook, stirring occasionally, for about 10 minutes, until lightly browned. Add the chicken, ground spices, garlic, ginger and lemon juice and stir-fry for 5 minutes.

3 Transfer to a casserole and top with the tomatoes. Add the coriander, yogurt and rice in layers. Drizzle over the saffron and milk, then 150ml/¼ pint/⅔ cup water.

4 Cover and bake for 1 hour. Transfer to a warmed serving platter and remove the whole spices. Garnish with toasted almonds and coriander and serve with yogurt.

Spatchcock of Poussin

Also called spring chicken, poussins are between four and six weeks old and weigh 350–600g/12oz–1¼ lb. The very young, smallest birds make an attractive serving for one person.

Serves 4
4 poussins

15ml/1 tbsp mixed chopped fresh
    herbs, such as rosemary and
    parsley, plus extra to garnish
15ml/1 tbsp lemon juice
50g/2oz/¼ cup butter, melted
salt and ground black pepper
lemon slices, to garnish
boiled new potatoes and salad,
    to serve (optional)

1 Remove any trussing strings from the birds and, using a pair of kitchen scissors, cut down on either side of the backbone. Lay the poussins flat, skin-side up, and flatten with the help of a rolling pin or mallet, or use the heel of your hand.

2 Thread the legs and wings on to skewers to keep the poussins flat while they are cooking.

3 Brush both sides with melted butter and season with salt and pepper. Sprinkle with lemon juice and herbs.

4 Preheat the grill (broiler) and cook, skin-side uppermost, for 6 minutes, until golden brown. Turn over, brush with more melted butter and grill (broil) for a further 6–8 minutes, until the juices run clear when the thickest part is pierced with the point of a sharp knife.

5 Transfer the poussins to serving plates and remove the skewers. Garnish with chopped herbs and lemon slices and serve immediately with boiled new potatoes and salad.

> **Variation**
> Squab, another very tender, young bird that provides an adequate single portion, is also ideal for this method of preparation and simple cooking.

Biryani Energy 628kcal/2623kJ; Protein 41.5g; Carbohydrate 71.4g, of which sugars 13.4g; Fat 19.7g, of which saturates 2.9g; Cholesterol 642mg; Calcium 163mg; Fibre 3.6g; Sodium 174mg.
Poussin Energy 621kcal/2582kJ; Protein 50.1g; Carbohydrate 0.3g, of which sugars 0.3g; Fat 46.7g, of which saturates 16.4g; Cholesterol 288mg; Calcium 21mg; Fibre 0g; Sodium 256mg.

Caribbean Chicken Kebabs

These kebabs have a rich, sunshine Caribbean flavour and the marinade keeps them moist without the need for oil.

Serves 4

500g/1¼lb skinless chicken
  breast fillets
finely grated rind of 1 lime
30ml/2 tbsp lime juice
15ml/1 tbsp rum or sherry
15g/½oz/1 tbsp light muscovado
  (brown) sugar
5ml/1 tsp ground cinnamon
2 mangoes, peeled, stoned (pitted)
  and diced
rice and salad, to serve

1 Cut the chicken into bitesize chunks and place in a non-metallic bowl with the lime rind and juice, rum or sherry, sugar and cinnamon. Toss well, cover with clear film (plastic wrap) and place in the refrigerator to marinate for 1 hour.

2 Preheat the grill (broiler). Drain the chicken, reserving the marinade. Thread the chicken on to four wooden skewers, alternating with the mango cubes.

3 Cook the skewers under the grill, turning occasionally and basting with the reserved marinade, for 8–10 minutes, until the chicken is tender and golden brown. Transfer to warmed plates and serve immediately with rice and salad.

Cook's Tips
• Mangoes have a large, flat, central stone (pit). The easiest way to prepare them is to cut the thickest possible lengthways slice from each side of the stone, then cut through the flesh in an even criss-cross pattern, leaving the skin intact. Turn the slice inside out so that the flesh stands up and cut it off the skin or scoop off the cubes with a spoon.
• Use a dark rum for the marinade to give a really rich and exotic flavour. However, if you don't like it – or the alternative of sherry – you can omit it. The kebabs will still taste delicious.
• Skinless boneless chicken thighs are a more economical alternative to breast portions.

Autumn Pheasant

Pheasant is worth buying as it is low in fat, full of flavour and never dry when cooked in this way.

Serves 4

1 oven-ready pheasant
2 small onions, quartered
3 celery sticks, thickly sliced
2 red eating apples, thickly sliced
120ml/4fl oz/½ cup stock
15ml/1 tbsp clear honey
30ml/2 tbsp Worcestershire sauce
pinch of freshly grated nutmeg
30ml/2 tbsp toasted hazelnuts
salt and ground black pepper

1 Preheat the oven to 180°C/350°F/Gas 4. Cook the pheasant without additional fat in a non-stick frying pan over medium-low heat, turning occasionally, for 8–10 minutes, until golden brown all over. Remove from the pan and keep hot.

2 Add the onions and celery to the pan, lower the heat and cook, stirring occasionally, for 8–10 minutes, until lightly browned. Spoon the vegetables into a casserole and place the pheasant on top. Tuck the apple slices around it.

3 Pour in the stock and add the honey and Worcestershire sauce. Sprinkle with nutmeg, season with salt and pepper, cover with a tight-fitting lid and bake for 1¼–1½ hours, or until tender. Sprinkle with the hazelnuts and serve immediately.

Cook's Tips
• Pheasant should be hung by the neck to develop its distinctive flavour for 7–14 days, depending on the degree of gaminess you like. After hanging, it must be plucked, cleaned and trussed.
• If you are buying the bird ready-prepared, it will almost certainly have already been hung. Make sure that all the tendons have been removed from the legs.
• This recipe provides an excellent method of cooking older cock birds, which tend to be rather tough and dry if they are just roasted. It is also a good choice for frozen birds as freezing has an adverse effect on their texture.

Chicken Stroganoff

This dish is based on the classic Russian dish (which is made with fillet of beef) and it is just as good.

Serves 4

4 skinless chicken breast fillets
45ml/3 tbsp olive oil
1 large onion, thinly sliced
225g/8oz mushrooms, sliced
300ml/½ pint/1¼ cups sour cream
salt and ground black pepper
15ml/1 tbsp chopped fresh parsley, to garnish

1 Divide the chicken into two natural fillets, place between two sheets of clear film (plastic wrap) and flatten each to a thickness of 5mm/¼in by beating lightly with the side of a rolling pin.

2 Remove the clear film and cut the meat into 2.5cm/1in strips diagonally across the fillets.

3 Heat 30ml/2 tbsp of the oil in a large frying pan over low heat. Add the onion and cook, stirring occasionally, for about 5 minutes, until softened but not coloured. Add the mushrooms and cook, stirring occasionally, for 5–8 minutes, until golden brown. Remove the onion and mushrooms and keep warm.

4 Increase the heat to medium and add the remaining oil to the pan. Add the chicken, in small batches, and cook, stirring frequently, for 3–4 minutes, until lightly coloured. Keep each batch warm while cooking the next.

5 Return all the chicken, onion and mushrooms to the pan and season with salt and pepper. Stir in the sour cream and bring to the boil. Sprinkle with fresh parsley and serve immediately.

Variation
Substitute smetana for the sour cream but do not let it boil as it will curdle. It is widely used in Russian cooking and is a good, low-fat substitute for cream.

Normandy Pheasant

Calvados, cider, apples and cream – the produce of Normandy – make this a rich and flavoursome dish.

Serves 4

2 oven-ready pheasants
15ml/1 tbsp olive oil
25g/1oz/2 tbsp butter
60ml/4 tbsp Calvados or applejack
450ml/¾ pint/scant 2 cups dry (hard) cider
1 bouquet garni
3 eating apples
150ml/¼ pint/⅔ cup double (heavy) cream
salt and ground black pepper
fresh thyme sprigs, to garnish

1 Preheat the oven to 160°C/325°F/Gas 3. Cut both pheasants into four pieces. Discard the backbones and knuckles.

2 Heat the oil and butter in a large flameproof casserole. Working in two batches, add the pheasant pieces to the casserole and brown them over a high heat. Return all the pheasant pieces to the casserole.

3 Standing well back, pour over the Calvados or applejack and ignite it with a match. Shake the casserole and when the flames have subsided, pour in the cider, then add the bouquet garni and season to taste with salt and pepper. Bring to the boil, cover with a tight-fitting lid and simmer for about 50 minutes.

4 Peel, core and thickly slice the apples. Tuck the apple slices around the pheasant. Cover and cook for 5–10 minutes, or until the pheasant is tender. Transfer the pheasant and apples to a warmed serving plate. Keep warm.

5 Remove and discard the bouquet garni, then boil the sauce rapidly to reduce by half to a syrupy consistency. Stir in the cream and simmer for a further 2–3 minutes, until thickened. Taste the sauce and adjust the seasoning, if necessary. Spoon the sauce over the pheasant pieces and serve immediately, garnished with fresh thyme sprigs.

Stroganoff Energy 421kcal/1758kJ; Protein 40.7g; Carbohydrate 9.8g, of which sugars 7.4g; Fat 24.7g, of which saturates 10.8g; Cholesterol 146mg; Calcium 103mg; Fibre 2g; Sodium 118mg.
Pheasant Energy 805kcal/3347kJ; Protein 58.8g; Carbohydrate 8.1g, of which sugars 8.1g; Fat 52.9g, of which saturates 24.6g; Cholesterol 525mg; Calcium 91mg; Fibre 0.8g; Sodium 191mg.

Roast Beef with Yorkshire Pudding

This classic British dish is often served at Sunday lunch, accompanied by potatoes, mustard and horseradish sauce.

Serves 6
1.75kg/4lb rib of beef
30–60ml/2–4 tbsp vegetable oil
300ml/½ pint/1¼ cups vegetable
   or veal stock, wine or water
salt and ground black pepper

For the puddings
50g/2oz/½ cup plain (all-
   purpose) flour
1 egg, beaten
150ml/¼ pint/⅔ cup water
   mixed with milk
vegetable oil, for cooking

1 Weigh the beef and calculate the cooking time. Allow 15 minutes per 450g/1lb plus 15 minutes for rare meat, 20 minutes plus 20 minutes for medium, and 25–30 minutes plus 25 minutes for well-done.

2 Preheat the oven to 220°C/425°F/Gas 7. Heat the oil in a roasting pan. Place the meat on a rack, fat-side uppermost, then put the rack in the roasting pan. Baste the beef with the oil and cook for the required time, basting occasionally.

3 To make the Yorkshire puddings, stir the flour, salt and pepper together in a bowl and form a well in the centre. Pour the egg into the well, then slowly pour in the milk mixture, stirring in the flour to give a smooth batter. Leave to stand for 30 minutes.

4 A few minutes before the meat is ready, spoon a little oil in each of 12 patty tins (muffin pans) and place in the oven until very hot. Remove the meat, season, then cover loosely with foil and keep warm. Quickly divide the batter among the patty tins, then bake for 15–20 minutes, until well risen and brown.

5 Spoon off the fat from the roasting pan. Add the stock, wine or water and bring to the boil, stirring constantly. Cook for a few minutes, stirring. Season to taste with salt and pepper, then serve with the beef and Yorkshire puddings.

Beef Olives

This British dish i so-called because of their shape, these beef rolls contain a delicious filling made with bacon, parsley and mushrooms.

Serves 4
25g/1oz/2 tbsp butter
2 rashers (strips) bacon,
   finely chopped
115g/4oz mushrooms, chopped
15ml/1 tbsp chopped fresh parsley
grated rind and juice of 1 lemon
115g/4oz/2 cups fresh
   white breadcrumbs
675g/1½lb topside (pot roast) of
   beef, cut into 8 thin slices
40g/1½oz/⅓ cup plain (all-
   purpose) flour
45ml/3 tbsp vegetable oil
2 onions, sliced
450ml/¾ pint/scant 2 cups
   brown veal stock
salt and ground black pepper

1 Preheat the oven to 160°C/325°F/Gas 3. Melt the butter in a pan over medium heat. Add the bacon and mushrooms and cook, stirring occasionally for 3 minutes. Mix them with the chopped parsley, lemon rind and juice and breadcrumbs in a bowl and season with salt and pepper.

2 Spread an equal quantity of the breadcrumb mixture evenly over the beef slices, leaving a narrow border clear around the edges. Roll up the slices and tie securely with fine string, then dip the beef rolls in the flour to coat lightly, shaking off any excess flour.

3 Heat the oil in a frying pan over medium heat. Add the beef rolls and cook, turning frequently, for 3–4 minutes, until evenly browned all over. Remove the rolls from the pan and keep warm. Add the onions and cook, stirring occasionally, for about 8 minutes, until browned. Stir in the remaining flour and cook until lightly browned. Pour in the stock, stirring constantly, bring to the boil, stirring, and simmer for 2–3 minutes.

4 Transfer the rolls to a casserole, pour the sauce over the top, then cover with a tight-fitting lid and cook in the oven for 2 hours. Lift out the "olives" using a slotted spoon and remove the string. Return them to the sauce and serve hot.

Roast Beef Energy 590kcal/2461kJ; Protein 68.5g; Carbohydrate 7.1g, of which sugars 0.7g; Fat 32g, of which saturates 11.9g; Cholesterol 202mg; Calcium 46mg; Fibre 0.3g; Sodium 204mg
Beef Olive Energy 519kcal/2181kJ; Protein 46.9g; Carbohydrate 38.1g, of which sugars 6.6g; Fat 21g, of which saturates 6.9g; Cholesterol 104mg; Calcium 90mg; Fibre 2.7g; Sodium 584mg.

Lamb & Spring Vegetable Stew

Known as a *blanquette* in France, this stew may have blanched asparagus spears or green beans added.

Serves 4

65g/2½oz/5 tbsp butter
900g/2lb lean boned shoulder of lamb, cut into 4cm/1½in dice
600ml/1 pint/2½ cups lamb stock or water
150ml/¼ pint/⅔ cup dry white wine
1 onion, quartered
2 fresh thyme sprigs
1 bay leaf
225g/8oz baby (pearl) onions, halved
225g/8oz young carrots
2 small turnips, quartered
175g/6oz/¾ cup shelled broad (fava) beans
15g/½oz/2 tbsp plain (all-purpose) flour
1 egg yolk
45ml/3 tbsp double (heavy) cream
10ml/2 tsp lemon juice
salt and ground black pepper
30ml/2 tbsp chopped fresh parsley, to garnish

1 Melt 25g/1oz/2 tbsp of the butter in a pan over medium heat. Add the lamb and cook, stirring frequently, for 8 minutes, until browned. Add the stock or water and wine, bring to the boil and skim the surface. Add the quartered onion, thyme and bay leaf. Lower the heat, cover the pan and simmer for 1 hour.

2 Melt 15g/½oz/1 tbsp of the remaining butter in a frying pan over low heat. Add the baby onions and cook, stirring occasionally, for about 10 minutes, until lightly browned all over. Add to the lamb with the carrots and turnips. Simmer for a further 20 minutes. Add the beans and cook for 10 minutes.

3 Arrange the lamb and vegetables on a serving dish, discarding the onion quarters and herbs. Cover and keep warm. Strain the stock and skim off the fat. Bring to the boil and reduce the stock to 450ml/¾ pint/scant 2 cups. Mix the remaining butter and flour to a paste. Whisk into the stock, then simmer briefly.

4 Combine the egg yolk and cream. Add a little of the hot sauce, then stir into the pan. Do not boil. Add the lemon juice, and season. Pour the sauce over the lamb and garnish with parsley.

Irish Stew

This wholesome and filling stew is given a slight piquancy by the inclusion of a little anchovy sauce.

Serves 4

4 rashers (strips) smoked streaky (fatty) bacon
2 celery sticks, chopped
2 large onions, sliced
8 middle neck (US shoulder) lamb chops (about 1kg/2¼lb total weight)
1kg/2¼lb potatoes, sliced
300ml/½ pint/1¼ cups brown veal stock
7.5ml/1½ tsp Worcestershire sauce
5ml/1 tsp anchovy sauce
salt and ground black pepper
fresh parsley, to garnish

1 Preheat the oven to 160°C/325°F/Gas 3. Dice the bacon and then cook in a heavy frying pan, without any added fat, over medium-low heat for 3–5 minutes, until the fat runs. Add the celery and one-third of the onions and cook, stirring occasionally, for about 10 minutes, until softened and browned.

2 Layer the lamb chops, potatoes, vegetable and bacon mixture and remaining onions in a heavy, flameproof casserole, seasoning each layer with salt and pepper as you go. Finish with a layer of potatoes.

3 Pour the veal stock, Worcestershire sauce and anchovy sauce into the bacon and vegetable cooking juices in the pan. Bring to the boil, stirring constantly. Pour the mixture into the casserole, adding water, if necessary, so that the liquid comes halfway up the sides of the casserole.

4 Cover the casserole with a tight-fitting lid, then cook in the oven for 3 hours, until the meat and vegetables are very tender. Return to the oven for longer if necessary. Serve immediately, sprinkled with chopped fresh parsley. Alternatively, leave to cool, then chill in the refrigerator overnight. Spoon off any fat that has solidified on the surface of the stew and reheat thoroughly in the oven or on the stove before serving.

Corned Beef & Egg Hash

This classic American hash is a perennially popular brunch dish and should be served with chilli sauce for an authentic touch.

Serves 4
30ml/2 tbsp vegetable oil
25g/1oz/2 tbsp butter
1 onion, finely chopped
1 small green (bell) pepper,
  seeded and diced

2 large boiled potatoes, diced
350g/12oz can corned beef, diced
1.5ml/¼ tsp freshly
  grated nutmeg
1.5ml/¼ tsp paprika
4 eggs
salt and ground black pepper
chopped fresh parsley, to garnish
chilli sauce, to serve

1 Heat the oil and butter in a large frying pan. Add the onion and cook, stirring occasionally, for 5–6 minutes until softened.

2 Mix together the green pepper, potatoes, corned beef, nutmeg and paprika in a bowl. Season with salt and pepper. Add to the pan and toss gently. Press down lightly and cook over a medium heat for 3–4 minutes, until a golden brown crust has formed on the underside.

3 Stir the mixture to distribute the crust, then repeat the process twice, until the mixture is well browned.

4 Make four wells in the hash and crack an egg into each one. Cover and cook gently for 4–5 minutes, until the egg whites are just set.

5 Sprinkle with chopped parsley and cut the hash into quarters. Serve immediately with chilli sauce.

> **Cook's Tip**
> Put the can of corned beef in the refrigerator for 30 minutes before using. It will firm up and you will be able to cut it into cubes more easily than if it is used at room temperature.

Best-ever American Burgers

These meaty quarter-pounders are far superior in both taste and texture to any burgers you can buy ready-made.

Makes 4 burgers
15ml/1 tbsp vegetable oil
1 small onion, chopped
450g/1lb minced (ground) beef
1 large garlic clove, crushed
5ml/1 tsp ground cumin
10ml/2 tsp ground coriander
30ml/2 tbsp tomato purée
  (paste) or ketchup

5ml/1 tsp wholegrain mustard
dash of Worcestershire sauce
30ml/2 tbsp mixed chopped fresh
  herbs, such as parsley, thyme
  and oregano or marjoram
15ml/1 tbsp lightly beaten egg
salt and ground black pepper
plain (all-purpose) flour,
  for shaping
vegetable oil, for frying (optional)
burger buns, mixed salad, chips
  (French fries) and relish, to
  serve

1 Heat the oil in a frying pan, Add the onion and cook, stirring occasionally, for 5 minutes, until softened. Remove from the pan, drain on kitchen paper and leave to cool.

2 Mix together the beef, garlic, spices, tomato purée or ketchup, mustard, Worcestershire sauce, herbs, beaten egg and seasoning in a bowl. Stir in the cooled onions.

3 Sprinkle a board with flour and shape the mixture into four burgers with floured hands and a spatula. Cover and chill in the refrigerator for 15 minutes.

4 Heat a little oil in a pan and fry the burgers over medium heat for about 5 minutes each side, depending on how rare you like them. Alternatively, cook under a medium grill (broiler) for the same time. Serve with buns, salad, chips and relish.

> **Cook's Tip**
> If you prefer, make eight smaller burgers to serve in buns, with melted cheese and tomato slices.

Burger Energy 298kcal/1237kJ; Protein 23.5g; Carbohydrate 2.3g, of which sugars 1.9g; Fat 21.7g, of which saturates 8.3g; Cholesterol 91mg; Calcium 20mg; Fibre 0.4g; Sodium 117mg.
Hash Energy 403kcal/1683kJ; Protein 30.4g; Carbohydrate 13g, of which sugars 5.1g; Fat 26.1g, of which saturates 10.5g; Cholesterol 277mg; Calcium 64mg; Fibre 1.4g; Sodium 868mg.

Bacon & Sausage Sauerkraut

Juniper berries and crushed coriander seeds flavour this traditional dish from Alsace.

Serves 4

30ml/2 tbsp vegetable oil
1 large onion, thinly sliced
1 garlic clove, crushed
450g/1lb bottled sauerkraut, rinsed and drained
1 eating apple, cored and chopped
5 juniper berries
5 coriander seeds, crushed
450g/1lb piece of lightly smoked bacon loin roast
225g/8oz whole smoked pork sausage, pricked
175ml/6fl oz/¾ cup unsweetened apple juice
150ml/¼ pint/⅔ cup chicken stock
1 bay leaf
8 small salad potatoes

1 Preheat the oven to 180°C/350°F/Gas 4. Heat the oil in a flameproof casserole over medium heat. Add the onion and garlic and cook, stirring occasionally, for 3–4 minutes, until softened but not coloured. Stir in the sauerkraut, apple, juniper berries and coriander seeds.

2 Lay the piece of bacon loin and the sausage on top of the sauerkraut, pour in the apple juice and stock, and add the bay leaf. Cover and bake in the oven for about 1 hour.

3 Remove from the oven and put the potatoes in the casserole. Add a little more stock if necessary, cover and bake for a further 30 minutes, or until the potatoes are tender.

4 Just before serving, lift out the bacon and sausages on to a board and slice. Spoon the sauerkraut on to a warmed platter, top with the meat and surround with the potatoes.

> **Cook's Tip**
> Sauerkraut is finely sliced, salted and fermented white cabbage. It is available in bottles and cans and, as it is pasteurized, it does not require the very long cooking times traditionally associated with this speciality.

Spiced Lamb with Apricots

Inspired by Middle Eastern cooking, this fruity, spicy casserole is simple to make yet looks impressive.

Serves 4

115g/4oz ready-to-eat dried apricots
50g/2oz/scant ½ cup seedless raisins
2.5ml/½ tsp saffron threads
150ml/¼ pint/⅔ cup orange juice
15ml/1 tbsp red wine vinegar
30–45ml/2–3 tbsp olive oil
1.5kg/3–3½ lb leg of lamb, boned and diced
1 onion, chopped
2 garlic cloves, crushed
10ml/2 tsp ground cumin
1.25ml/¼ tsp ground cloves
15ml/1 tbsp ground coriander
25g/1oz/¼ cup plain (all-purpose) flour
600ml/1 pint/2½ cups lamb or chicken stock
45ml/3 tbsp chopped fresh coriander (cilantro)
salt and ground black pepper
saffron rice mixed with toasted almonds and chopped fresh coriander, to serve

1 Mix together the dried apricots, raisins, saffron, orange juice and vinegar in a bowl. Cover with clear film (plastic wrap) and leave to soak for 2–3 hours.

2 Preheat the oven to 160°C/325°F/Gas 3. Heat 30ml/2 tbsp oil in a large flameproof casserole over medium heat. Add the lamb, in batches, and cook, stirring frequently, for 5–8 minutes, until evenly browned. Remove and set aside.

3 Add a little more oil to the casserole, if necessary, and lower the heat. Add the onion and garlic and cook, stirring occasionally, for 5 minutes, until softened but not coloured.

4 Stir in the spices and flour and cook for 1–2 minutes more. Return the meat to the casserole. Stir in the stock, fresh coriander and the soaked fruit with its liquid. Season to taste with salt and pepper, then bring to the boil. Cover the casserole with a tight-fitting lid and simmer for 1½ hours (adding extra stock if necessary), or until the lamb is tender. Serve with saffron rice mixed with toasted almonds and fresh coriander.

Sauerkraut Energy 562kcal/2347kJ; Protein 42.6g; Carbohydrate 31.8g, of which sugars 14.4g; Fat 30.2g, of which saturates 10g; Cholesterol 49mg; Calcium 118mg; Fibre 5.1g; Sodium 2352mg.
Lamb Energy 765kcal/3192kJ; Protein 58.5g; Carbohydrate 27.5g, of which sugars 23.4g; Fat 47.5g, of which saturates 14.7g; Cholesterol 218mg; Calcium 53mg; Fibre 2.5g; Sodium 181mg.

Beef Wellington

This English dish is so-
named because of a
supposed resemblance in
shape and colour to the
Duke of Wellington's boot.

Serves 8
1.4kg/3lb fillet (tenderloin) of beef
15g/½oz/1 tbsp butter
30ml/2 tbsp vegetable oil

½ small onion, finely chopped
175g/6oz mushrooms, chopped
175g/6oz liver pâté
freshly squeezed lemon juice
a few drops of Worcestershire
  sauce
400g/14oz puff pastry dough,
  thawed if frozen
beaten egg, to glaze
salt and ground black pepper

1 Preheat the oven to 220°C/425°F/Gas 7. Season the beef
with pepper, then tie it at intervals with string.

2 Heat the butter and oil in a roasting pan over high heat.
Add the beef and cook, turning frequently, for 8–10 minutes,
until evenly browned all over. Transfer the roasting pan to the
oven and cook for 20 minutes. Remove the beef from the
oven, transfer to a plate and leave to cool. Remove and discard
the string.

3 Meanwhile, scrape the cooking juices into a pan, add the
onion and mushrooms and cook over low heat, stirring
occasionally, for about 5 minutes, until the onion is softened but
not coloured. Leave to cool, then mix with the pâté. Add the
lemon juice and Worcestershire sauce. Preheat the oven again
to 220°C/425°F/Gas 7.

4 Roll out the pastry dough to a large rectangle 5mm/¼in
thick. Spread the pâté mixture on the beef, then place it in the
centre of the dough. Dampen the edges of the dough, then fold
it over the beef to make a neat parcel, tucking in the ends tidily.
Press firmly to seal.

5 Place the parcel on a baking sheet with the join underneath
and brush with beaten egg. Bake in the oven for 25–45
minutes, depending how well done you like the beef. Serve in
generous slices.

Butterflied Cumin & Garlic Lamb

Ground cumin and garlic
give the lamb a wonderful
Middle-Eastern flavour.

Serves 6
1.75kg/4lb leg of lamb
60ml/4 tbsp extra virgin olive oil

30ml/2 tbsp ground cumin
4–6 garlic cloves, crushed
salt and ground black pepper
toasted almond and raisin rice,
  to serve
fresh coriander (cilantro) sprigs
  and lemon wedges, to garnish

1 To butterfly the lamb, cut away the meat from the bone using
a small sharp knife. Remove any excess fat and the thin,
parchment-like membrane. Flatten the meat with a rolling pin
to an even thickness, then prick the fleshy side of the lamb well
with the tip of a knife. Place the lamb in a large, shallow dish.

2 Mix together the olive oil, cumin and garlic in a bowl and
season with pepper. Spoon the mixture all over the lamb, then
rub it well into the crevices. Cover the dish with clear film
(plastic wrap) and place the lamb in the refrigerator to
marinate overnight.

3 Preheat the oven to 200°C/400°F/Gas 6. Spread the lamb,
skin side down, on a rack in a roasting pan. Season with salt and
roast for 45–60 minutes, until crusty brown on the outside but
still pink in the centre.

4 Remove the lamb from the roasting pan and place on a
board. Cover with foil and leave it to rest for about 10 minutes.
Cut into diagonal slices, place on warmed plates and serve
immediately with the toasted almond and raisin rice. Garnish
with fresh coriander sprigs and lemon wedges.

Cook's Tip
The lamb may be cooked on the barbecue rather than
roasted in the oven. Thread it on to two long skewers and
grill over hot coals for 20–25 minutes on each side, until it is
cooked to your liking.

Beef Energy 511kcal/2131kJ; Protein 41.7g; Carbohydrate 19.3g, of which sugars 1.2g; Fat 30.6g, of which saturates 7.2g; Cholesterol 128mg; Calcium 41mg; Fibre 0.4g; Sodium 320mg.
Lamb Energy 505kcal/2106kJ; Protein 59.8g; Carbohydrate 0g, of which sugars 0g; Fat 29.5g, of which saturates 12.8g; Cholesterol 225mg; Calcium 23mg; Fibre 0g; Sodium 128mg.

Pork with Mozzarella & Sage

Here is a variation of the famous dish *saltimbocca alla romana* – the mozzarella cheese adds a delicious creamy flavour.

Serves 2–3

225g/8oz pork fillet (tenderloin)
1 garlic clove, crushed
75g/3oz mozzarella cheese, cut
    into 6 slices
6 slices prosciutto
6 large sage leaves
25g/1oz/2 tbsp butter
salt and ground black pepper
potato wedges roasted in olive oil
    and green beans, to serve

1 Trim any excess fat from the pork, then cut the meat crossways into six pieces about 2.5cm/1in thick.

2 Stand each piece of pork on its end and flatten by beating with the side of a rolling pin. Rub each piece with garlic, place on a plate, cover with clear film (plastic wrap) and set aside for 30 minutes in a cool place.

3 Place a slice of mozzarella on top of each piece of pork and season with salt and pepper. Lay a slice of prosciutto on top of each, crinkling it a little to fit. Press a sage leaf on to each and secure with a wooden cocktail stick (toothpick).

4 Melt the butter in a large, heavy frying pan. Add the pieces of pork and cook for about 2 minutes on each side, until the mozzarella begins to melt. Remove and discard the cocktail sticks, divide the pork among warmed serving plates and serve immediately with roasted potatoes and green beans.

Cook's Tips
• The original saltimbocca, which means "jump in the mouth", was made with veal escalopes (US scallops) and there is no reason why you should not also use these for this variation.
• Try to find traditional mozzarella made with buffalo rather than cow's milk, as it has a better flavour and more delicate texture when melted.

Five-spice Lamb

This aromatic lamb casserole is a perfect dish to serve at an informal lunch or supper party.

Serves 4

30–45ml/2–3 tbsp vegetable oil
1.5kg/3–3½lb leg of lamb, boned
    and diced
1 onion, chopped
10ml/2 tsp grated fresh
    root ginger
1 garlic clove, crushed
5ml/1 tsp Chinese five-
    spice powder
30ml/2 tbsp hoisin sauce
15ml/1 tbsp soy sauce
300ml/½ pint/1¼ cups passata
    (bottled strained tomatoes)
250ml/8fl oz/1 cup lamb or
    chicken stock
1 red (bell) pepper, seeded
    and diced
1 yellow (bell) pepper, seeded
    and diced
30ml/2 tbsp chopped fresh
    coriander (cilantro)
15ml/1 tbsp sesame
    seeds, toasted
salt and ground black pepper
boiled rice, to serve

1 Preheat the oven to 160°C/325°F/Gas 3. Heat 30ml/2 tbsp of the oil in a large, flameproof casserole. Add the lamb, in batches, and cook over high heat, stirring frequently, until evenly browned. Remove to a plate and set aside.

2 Add the onion, ginger and garlic to the casserole with a little more of the oil, if necessary. Lower the heat and cook, stirring occasionally, for 5 minutes, until softened but not coloured.

3 Return the lamb to the casserole. Stir in the five-spice powder, hoisin sauce, soy sauce, passata and stock and season to taste with salt and pepper. Bring to the boil, then cover with a tight-fitting lid and cook in the oven for about 1¼ hours.

4 Remove the casserole from the oven and stir in the red and yellow peppers. Cover the casserole again and return to the oven for a further 15 minutes, or until the lamb is very tender.

5 Sprinkle with the chopped fresh coriander and toasted sesame seeds. Spoon on to warmed, individual plates and serve immediately accompanied by rice, if you like.

Pork Energy 245kcal/1018kJ; Protein 25.3g; Carbohydrate 0.3g, of which sugars 0.3g; Fat 15.8g, of which saturates 9.1g; Cholesterol 94mg; Calcium 99mg; Fibre 0g; Sodium 502mg.
Lamb Energy 453kcal/1892kJ; Protein 39.2g; Carbohydrate 9.4g, of which sugars 8.7g; Fat 29.1g, of which saturates 10.9g; Cholesterol 143mg; Calcium 59mg; Fibre 2.4g; Sodium 606mg.

Indian Curried Lamb Samosas

Authentic samosa pastry is difficult to make but these samosas work equally well using puff pastry.

Serves 4

15ml/1 tbsp vegetable oil
1 garlic clove, crushed
175g/6oz minced (ground) lamb
4 spring onions (scallions), finely chopped
10ml/2 tsp medium-hot curry paste
4 ready-to-eat dried apricots, chopped
1 small potato, diced
10ml/2 tsp apricot chutney
30ml/2 tbsp frozen peas
squeeze of lemon juice
15ml/1 tbsp chopped fresh coriander (cilantro)
225g/8oz puff pastry dough, thawed if frozen
beaten egg, to glaze
5ml/1 tsp cumin seeds
salt and ground black pepper
45ml/3 tbsp natural (plain) yogurt with chopped fresh mint, to serve
fresh mint sprigs, to garnish

1 Preheat the oven to 220°C/425°F/Gas 7 and dampen a large non-stick baking sheet. Heat the oil in a pan over medium heat and cook the garlic for 30 seconds, then add the lamb. Cook, stirring frequently, for about 5 minutes, until the meat is well browned.

2 Stir in the spring onions, curry paste, apricots and potato, and cook for 2–3 minutes. Then add the chutney, peas and 60ml/ 4 tbsp water. Cover and simmer for 10 minutes, stirring occasionally. Stir in the lemon juice and coriander, season to taste with salt and pepper, remove and leave to cool.

3 Roll out the pastry and cut into four 15cm/6in squares. Place a quarter of the curry mixture in the centre of each square and brush the edges with beaten egg. Fold over to make a triangle and seal the edges. Knock up the edges with the back of a knife and make a small slit in the top of each.

4 Brush each samosa with beaten egg and sprinkle with the cumin seeds. Place on the damp baking sheet and bake for about 20 minutes. Serve garnished with mint sprigs and with the minty yogurt handed separately.

Breton Pork & Bean Casserole

This is a traditional French dish, called *cassoulet*. There are many variations in the different regions of France.

Serves 4

30ml/2 tbsp olive oil
1 onion, chopped
2 garlic cloves, chopped
450g/1lb pork shoulder, diced
350g/12oz lean lamb (preferably leg), diced
225g/8oz coarse pork and garlic sausage, cut into chunks
400g/14oz can chopped tomatoes
30ml/2 tbsp red wine
15ml/1 tbsp tomato purée (paste)
1 bouquet garni
400g/14oz can cannellini beans, drained and rinsed
50g/2oz/1 cup fresh brown breadcrumbs
salt and ground black pepper
green salad and French bread, to serve

1 Preheat the oven to 160°C/325°F/Gas 3. Heat the oil in a large flameproof casserole over low heat. Add the onion and garlic and cook, stirring occasionally, for about 5 minutes, until softened but not coloured. Remove with a slotted spoon and set aside on a plate.

2 Add the pork, lamb and sausage chunks to the casserole, increase the heat to high and cook, stirring frequently, for about 8 minutes, until evenly browned. Return the onion and garlic to the casserole.

3 Stir in the chopped tomatoes, wine and tomato purée and add 300ml/½ pint/1¼ cups water. Season to taste with salt and pepper and add the bouquet garni. Cover with a tight-fitting lid and bring to the boil, then transfer the casserole to the oven and cook for 1½ hours.

4 Remove and discard the bouquet garni. Stir in the cannellini beans and sprinkle the breadcrumbs over the top. Return the casserole to the oven and cook, uncovered, for a further 30 minutes, until the meat is tender and the topping is golden brown. Serve immediately with a green salad and French bread to mop up the juices.

Samosas Energy 392kcal/1642kJ; Protein 13.7g; Carbohydrate 36.8g, of which sugars 12.4g; Fat 22.7g, of which saturates 3.2g; Cholesterol 34mg; Calcium 66mg; Fibre 2.3g; Sodium 212mg.
Casserole Energy 724kcal/3030kJ; Protein 56.6g; Carbohydrate 37.7g, of which sugars 9.2g; Fat 39g, of which saturates 14g; Cholesterol 164mg; Calcium 138mg; Fibre 8.1g; Sodium 1086mg.

Pan-fried Mediterranean Lamb

The warm, summery flavours of the Mediterranean are combined for a simple weekday meal.

Serves 4

8 lean lamb cutlets
  (US rib chops)
1 onion, thinly sliced
2 red (bell) peppers, seeded
  and sliced
400g/14oz can plum tomatoes
1 garlic clove, crushed
45ml/3 tbsp chopped fresh basil
30ml/2 tbsp chopped pitted
  black olives
salt and ground black pepper
pasta, to serve (optional)

1 Trim any excess fat from the lamb, then cook in a non-stick frying pan, without any added fat, turning frequently, for 4–5 minutes, until golden brown all over.

2 Add the onion and red peppers to the pan. Cook, stirring, for a few minutes to soften, then add the plum tomatoes, garlic and fresh basil leaves.

3 Cover and simmer for 20 minutes, or until the lamb is tender. Stir in the olives, season to taste with salt and pepper and serve hot, with pasta if you like.

Cook's Tip
Lamb cutlets (US rib chops) are much thinner than chops taken from the loin and it is necessary to cut off the fat before cooking. However, they are less expensive than chops and the meat has a very sweet flavour.

Variations
• The red (bell) peppers give this dish a slightly sweet taste. If you prefer, use green peppers for a more savoury stew.
• Substitute sliced green olives stuffed with pimiento for the chopped black ones.

Greek Lamb Pie

Ready-made filo pastry is so easy to use and gives a most professional look to this lamb and spinach pie.

Serves 4

sunflower oil, for brushing
450g/1lb minced (ground) lamb
1 onion, sliced
1 garlic clove, crushed
400g/14oz can plum tomatoes
30ml/2 tbsp chopped fresh mint
5ml/1 tsp freshly grated nutmeg
350g/12oz young spinach leaves
275g/10oz filo pastry, thawed if
  frozen
5ml/1 tsp sesame seeds
salt and ground black pepper
green salad or vegetables,
  to serve (optional)

1 Preheat the oven to 200°C/400°F/Gas 6. Lightly oil a 22cm/8½in round springform tin (pan).

2 Cook the lamb and onion, without any added fat, in a non-stick pan over medium heat, stirring frequently, for about 5 minutes, until the meat is golden brown.

3 Stir in the garlic, tomatoes with their can juices, mint and nutmeg and season with salt and pepper. Bring to the boil, stirring occasionally. Lower the heat and simmer gently, stirring occasionally, until most of the liquid has evaporated. Remove the pan from the heat and leave to cool.

4 Wash the spinach and remove any tough stalks, then cook in a large pan with only the water clinging to the leaves for about 2 minutes, until just wilted. Drain well, squeezing out as much liquid as possible.

5 Lightly brush each sheet of filo pastry with oil and lay in overlapping layers in the prepared tin, leaving enough pastry overhanging the sides to wrap over the top.

6 Spoon in the meat mixture and spinach, then wrap the pastry over to enclose, scrunching it slightly. Lightly brush the top of the pie with oil, sprinkle with sesame seeds and bake for about 25–30 minutes, or until golden and crisp. Serve hot, with a green salad or vegetables.

Pan-Fried Energy 637kcal/2634kJ; Protein 23.9g; Carbohydrate 9.9g, of which sugars 9.3g; Fat 56g, of which saturates 27.3g; Cholesterol 117mg; Calcium 33mg; Fibre 2.8g; Sodium 272mg.
Lamb Pie Energy 446kcal/1872kJ; Protein 29.2g; Carbohydrate 39.7g, of which sugars 5.9g; Fat 20g, of which saturates 7.7g; Cholesterol 87mg; Calcium 248mg; Fibre 4.5g; Sodium 211mg.

Pasta Carbonara

This classic Roman dish is traditionally made with spaghetti, but is equally good with fresh egg tagliatelle.

Serves 4
350–450g/12oz–1lb fresh
  tagliatelle pasta
15ml/1 tbsp olive oil
225g/8oz piece of ham or bacon,
  cut into 2.5cm/1in sticks
115g/4oz button mushrooms,
  sliced
4 eggs, lightly beaten
75ml/5 tbsp single (light) cream
30ml/2 tbsp finely grated
  Parmesan cheese
salt and ground black pepper
fresh basil sprigs or parsley, to
  garnish

1 Bring a large pan of lightly salted water to the boil, add a little oil and cook the tagliatelle for 6–8 minutes or until *al dente*.

2 Meanwhile, heat the oil in a frying pan and cook the ham for 3–4 minutes, then add the mushrooms and fry for a further 3–4 minutes. Turn off the heat and set the pan aside. Lightly beat the eggs and cream together in a bowl and season well with salt and pepper.

3 When the pasta is cooked, drain it well and return to the pan. Add the ham, mushrooms and any pan juices and stir well into the pasta.

4 Pour in the egg and cream mixture, together with half the Parmesan cheese. Stir well – as you do this the eggs will cook in the heat of the pasta. Pile on to warmed serving plates, sprinkle with the remaining Parmesan and garnish with basil leaves or parsley. Serve immediately.

> **Cook's Tip**
> *For an authentic Italian flavour, use slices of pancetta. Made from pork belly, it is cured in salt and spices to give it a delicious taste. Pancetta is sold at Italian delicatessens and is now increasingly available from larger supermarkets.*

Lasagne

Serve with a mixed salad and crusty bread for a tasty supper with friends.

Serves 8
1 large onion, chopped
2 garlic cloves, crushed
500g/1¼lb extra-lean minced
  (ground) beef or turkey
450ml/¾ pint/scant 2 cups
  passata (bottled strained
  tomatoes)
5ml/1 tsp mixed dried herbs
225g/8oz frozen spinach, thawed
200g/7oz lasagne verdi
200g/7oz cottage cheese
mixed salad, to serve

For the sauce
25g/1oz/2 tbsp half-fat spread
25g/1oz/¼ cup plain (all-purpose)
  flour
300ml/½ pint/1¼ cups skimmed
  milk
1.5ml/¼ tsp freshly grated
  nutmeg
25g/1oz/⅓ cup freshly grated
  Parmesan cheese
salt and ground black pepper

1 Put the onion, garlic and beef or turkey in a non-stick pan. Cook quickly, stirring with a wooden spoon to separate the pieces, for 5 minutes, or until the meat is browned all over.

2 Add the passata, dried herbs and seasoning and stir to mix. Bring to the boil, then reduce the heat, cover and simmer, stirring occasionally, for about 30 minutes.

3 Meanwhile, make the sauce. Put all the sauce ingredients, except the Parmesan cheese, into a pan. Cook gently, whisking continuously, until the sauce thickens and is bubbling and smooth. Remove from the heat. Adjust the seasoning to taste, add the Parmesan cheese to the sauce and stir to mix.

4 Preheat the oven to 190°C/375°F/Gas 5. Arrange the spinach leaves on sheets of kitchen paper and pat them until dry.

5 Layer the meat mixture, lasagne, cottage cheese and spinach in a 2 litre/3½ pint/8 cup ovenproof dish, starting and ending with a layer of meat mixture. Spoon the cheese sauce evenly over the top to cover the meat completely, then bake in the oven for 40–50 minutes, or until bubbling.

Carbonara Energy 535kcal/2257kJ; Protein 31.7g; Carbohydrate 66g, of which sugars 4g; Fat 18.1g, of which saturates 6.6g; Cholesterol 241mg; Calcium 165mg; Fibre 3.2g; Sodium 838mg.
Lasagne Energy 279kcal/1173kJ; Protein 21.9g; Carbohydrate 27.4g, of which sugars 6.7g; Fat 9.8g, of which saturates 4g; Cholesterol 38mg; Calcium 180mg; Fibre 2.3g; Sodium 183mg.

Mushroom & Pancetta Pizzas

Try to use a mix of wild and cultivated mushrooms to give these individual pizzas lots of earthy flavour.

Serves 4

I quantity Basic Pizza Dough (see page 158)
60ml/4 tbsp olive oil
2 garlic cloves, crushed
225g/8oz fresh mixed ceps and chestnut mushrooms, roughly chopped
75g/3oz pancetta, roughly chopped
15ml/1 tbsp chopped fresh oregano
45ml/3 tbsp freshly grated Parmesan cheese
salt and ground black pepper

1 Preheat the oven to 220°C/425°F/Gas 7. Divide the dough into four pieces and roll out each one on a lightly floured surface to a 13cm/5in circle. Place well apart on two greased baking sheets.

2 Heat 30ml/2 tbsp of the olive oil in a frying pan and fry the garlic and mushrooms gently until the mushrooms are tender and the juices have evaporated. Season to taste with salt and pepper, then cool.

3 Brush the pizza bases with 15ml/1 tbsp oil, then spoon over the mushrooms. Scatter over the pancetta and oregano.

4 Sprinkle the toppings with grated Parmesan cheese and drizzle over the remaining oil. Bake for 10–15 minutes, until crisp. Serve immediately.

> **Cook's Tip**
> • Pancetta is available in larger supermarkets and Italian delicatessens. If you have difficulty finding it, use chopped slices of streaky (fatty) bacon in its place.
> • If fresh ceps are not available, you can add extra flavour to cultivated mushrooms by adding some dried porcini mushrooms, which are sold in larger supermarkets. Soak them in hot water for 20 minutes until soft before adding to the pan in step 2.

Pepperoni Pizza

This classic pizza is sure to go down well with family and friends alike. Who can resist a slice of home-made pizza, topped with a luscious combination of tangy pepperoni and lashings of cheese?

Serves 4
For the sauce
30ml/2 tbsp olive oil
1 onion, finely chopped
1 garlic clove, crushed
400g/14oz can chopped tomatoes with herbs
15ml/1 tbsp tomato purée (paste)

For the pizza base
275g/10oz/2½ cups plain (all-purpose) flour
2.5ml/½ tsp salt
5ml/1 tsp easy-blend (rapid-rise) dried yeast
30ml/2 tbsp olive oil

For the topping
150g/5oz mozzarella cheese, sliced
75g/3oz pepperoni sausage, thinly sliced
½ each red, yellow and green (bell) pepper, sliced (optional)
8 black olives, pitted
3 sun-dried tomatoes, chopped
2.5ml/½ tsp dried oregano
olive oil, for drizzling

1 To make the sauce, heat the oil and fry the onions and garlic until softened. Add the tomatoes and tomato purée, then boil rapidly for 5 minutes until reduced slightly. Leave to cool.

2 To make the pizza base, sift the flour and salt into a bowl. Sprinkle over the yeast and make a well in the centre. Pour in 175ml/6fl oz/¾ cup warm water and the olive oil. Mix to a soft dough. Knead the dough on a lightly floured surface for about 5–10 minutes until smooth. Roll out to a 25cm/10in round, press up the edges slightly and place on a greased baking sheet.

3 Spread over the tomato sauce and top with the peppers, if using, mozzarella, pepperoni, olives and sun-dried tomatoes. Sprinkle over the oregano and drizzle with olive oil.

4 Cover loosely and leave in a warm place for 30 minutes. Meanwhile, preheat the oven to 220°C/425°F/ Gas 7. Bake for 25–30 minutes, then serve.

Mushroom Energy 344kcal/1435kJ; Protein 12g; Carbohydrate 27g, of which sugars 1.7g; Fat 21.6g, of which saturates 5.5g; Cholesterol 23mg; Calcium 180mg; Fibre 1.6g; Sodium 488mg.
Pepperoni Energy 521kcal/2184kJ; Protein 17.5g; Carbohydrate 62.4g, of which sugars 8.6g; Fat 24g, of which saturates 8.2g; Cholesterol 43mg; Calcium 256mg; Fibre 4.7g; Sodium 484mg.

Hungarian Beef Goulash

Spicy beef stew served with caraway flavoured dumplings will satisfy even the hungriest Hungarian.

Serves 4
30ml/2 tbsp vegetable oil
1 kg/2lb braising steak, diced
2 onions, chopped
1 garlic clove, crushed
15g/½oz/2 tbsp plain (all-purpose) flour
10ml/2 tsp paprika
5ml/1 tsp caraway seeds
400g/14oz can
    chopped tomatoes

300ml/½ pint/1¼ cups beef stock
1 large carrot, chopped
1 red (bell) pepper, seeded and chopped
salt and ground black pepper
sour cream, to serve
pinch of paprika, to garnish

For the dumplings
115g/4oz/1 cup self-raising (self-rising) flour
40g/2oz/½ cup shredded suet
15ml/1 tbsp chopped fresh parsley
2.5ml/½ tsp caraway seeds

1 Heat the oil in a flameproof casserole over high heat. Add the meat and cook, stirring frequently, for 5 minutes, until evenly browned. Remove with a slotted spoon.

2 Lower the heat, add the onions and garlic and cook, stirring occasionally, for about 5 minutes, until softened but not coloured. Stir in the flour, paprika and caraway seeds and cook, stirring constantly, for 2 minutes.

3 Return the meat to the casserole and stir in the tomatoes and stock. Bring to the boil, cover and simmer for 2 hours.

4 To make the dumplings, sift the flour and seasoning into a bowl, add the suet, parsley, caraway seeds and 45–60ml/ 3–4 tbsp water and mix to a soft dough. Divide into eight pieces and roll into balls. Cover and set aside.

5 After 2 hours, stir the carrot and red pepper into the goulash, and season. Drop the dumplings into the casserole, cover and simmer for a further 25 minutes. Serve in bowls topped with a spoonful of sour cream sprinkled with paprika.

Pork Satay with Peanut Sauce

These delightful little satay sticks from Thailand make a good light meal or a drinks party snack.

Makes 8
½ small onion, chopped
2 garlic cloves, crushed
30ml/2 tbsp lemon juice
15ml/1 tbsp soy sauce
5ml/1 tsp ground coriander
2.5ml/½ tsp ground cumin
5ml/1 tsp ground turmeric
30ml/2 tbsp vegetable oil
450g/1lb pork fillet (tenderloin)
salt and ground black pepper
fresh coriander (cilantro) sprigs, to garnish
boiled rice, to serve

For the sauce
150ml/¼ pint/⅔ cup coconut cream
60ml/4 tbsp crunchy peanut butter
15ml/1 tbsp lemon juice
2.5ml/½ tsp ground cumin
2.5ml/½ tsp ground coriander
5ml/1 tsp soft brown sugar
15ml/1 tbsp soy sauce
1–2 dried red chillies, seeded and chopped
15ml/1 tbsp chopped fresh coriander

For the salad
½ small cucumber, peeled and diced
15ml/1 tbsp white wine vinegar
15ml/1 tbsp chopped fresh coriander

1 Put the onion, garlic, lemon juice, soy sauce, ground coriander, cumin, turmeric and oil in a food processor and process until smooth. Cut the pork into strips, mix with the spice marinade in a bowl, cover with clear film (plastic wrap) and chill.

2 Preheat the grill (broiler). Thread two or three pork pieces on to each of eight soaked wooden skewers and grill (broil) for 2–3 minutes on each side, basting with the marinade.

3 To make the sauce, put all the ingredients into a pan, bring to the boil, stirring constantly, and simmer for 5 minutes.

4 Mix together all the salad ingredients. Arrange the satay sticks on a platter, garnish with coriander sprigs and season. Serve immediately with the sauce and boiled rice.

Goulash Energy 751kcal/3136kJ; Protein 62.1g; Carbohydrate 41.2g, of which sugars 13.2g; Fat 38.9g, of which saturates 15.4g; Cholesterol 153mg; Calcium 159mg; Fibre 4.6g; Sodium 282mg.
Satay Energy 189kcal/784kJ; Protein 14.5g; Carbohydrate 2.9g, of which sugars 2.2g; Fat 13.3g, of which saturates 5.8g; Cholesterol 35mg; Calcium 25mg; Fibre 0.9g; Sodium 70mg.

Sizzling Beef with Celeriac Straw

The crisp celeriac batons look like fine pieces of straw when cooked and have a mild celery-like flavour.

Serves 4

450g/1lb celeriac
150ml/¼ pint/⅔ cup
   vegetable oil
1 red (bell) pepper
6 spring onions (scallions)
450g/1lb rump (round) steak
60ml/4 tbsp beef stock
30ml/2 tbsp sherry vinegar
10ml/2 tsp Worcestershire sauce
10ml/2 tsp tomato
   purée (paste)
salt and ground black pepper

1 Peel the celeriac and then cut it into fine batons, using a cleaver if you have one or a large sharp knife.

2 Heat a wok, then add two-thirds of the oil. When the oil is hot, add the celeriac batons, in batches, and stir-fry until golden brown and crisp. Drain well on kitchen paper. Discard the oil.

3 Seed the red pepper and cut it and the spring onions into 2.5cm/1in lengths, cutting diagonally. Cut the steak into strips, across the grain of the meat.

4 Heat the wok again, then add the remaining oil. When the oil is hot, add the red pepper and spring onions and stir-fry for 2–3 minutes.

5 Add the steak strips and stir-fry for a further 3–4 minutes, until well browned. Add the stock, vinegar, Worcestershire sauce and tomato purée. Season well with salt and pepper and serve with the celeriac "straw".

> **Cook's Tip**
> The Chinese use a large cleaver for preparing most vegetables. With a little practice, you will discover that it is the ideal kitchen utensil for cutting fine vegetable batons and chopping thin strips of meat.

Stir-fried Pork with Lychees

No extra oil or fat is needed to cook this Chinese-style dish, as the pork produces enough on its own.

Serves 4

450g/1lb fatty pork, such as belly pork, with the skin on or off
30ml/2 tbsp hoisin sauce
4 spring onions (scallions),
   sliced diagonally
175g/6oz lychees, peeled, stoned
   (pitted) and cut into slivers
salt and ground black pepper
fresh lychees and parsley sprigs,
   to garnish

1 Cut the pork into bitesize pieces and place in a dish. Pour the hoisin sauce over it and toss to coat. Cover with clear film (plastic wrap) and leave to marinate in a cool place for at least 30 minutes.

2 Heat a wok, then add the pork and stir-fry for 5 minutes, until crisp and golden. Add the spring onions and stir-fry for a further 2 minutes.

3 Sprinkle the lychee slivers over the pork, and season well with salt and pepper. Transfer to warmed plates, garnish with lychees and parsley sprigs and serve immediately.

> **Cook's Tip**
> Lychees have a very pretty pink skin which cracks easily when the fruit is pressed between finger and thumb, making them easy to peel. The fruit is a soft, fleshy berry and contains a long, shiny, brown seed. This is inedible and must be removed. The sweet flesh is pearly white and fragrant, similar in texture to a grape. When buying lychees, avoid any that are turning brown, as they will be over-ripe. Equally, avoid under-ripe lychees with green or beige skins. Look for fruit with as much red or pink in the skins as possible. Fresh lychees are delicate and should be used as soon after purchase as possible, but can be stored in the refrigerator for up to a week. If you cannot buy the fresh fruit, you could use drained canned lychees, but they do not have the same fragrance or flavour.

Pork Energy 465kcal/1926kJ; Protein 17.9g; Carbohydrate 8.7g, of which sugars 8.6g; Fat 40.1g, of which saturates 14.8g; Cholesterol 81mg; Calcium 17mg; Fibre 0.5g; Sodium 206mg.
Beef Energy 318kcal/1324kJ; Protein 26.2g; Carbohydrate 5g, of which sugars 4.8g; Fat 21.6g, of which saturates 3.9g; Cholesterol 66mg; Calcium 66mg; Fibre 2.2g; Sodium 174mg.

Sukiyaki-style Beef

This dish incorporates all the traditional Japanese elements – meat, vegetables, noodles and tofu.

Serves 4

450g/1lb thick rump (round) steak
200g/7oz/3½ cups Japanese rice noodles
15ml/1 tbsp shredded suet
200g/7oz firm tofu, cut into dice

8 shiitake mushrooms, trimmed
2 leeks, sliced into 2.5cm/ 1in lengths
90g/3½ oz/scant 1 cup baby spinach, to serve

For the stock

15g/½oz/1 tbsp caster (superfine) sugar
90ml/6 tbsp rice wine
45ml/3 tbsp dark soy sauce
120ml/4fl oz/½ cup water

1 If there is time, chill the steak in the freezer for 30 minutes to make it easier to slice thinly. Cut the steak into thin even-size slices with a very sharp knife.

2 Blanch the rice noodles in a large pan of boiling water for 2 minutes, then drain well.

3 Mix together all the ingredients for the stock in a bowl, stirring until the sugar has dissolved. Set aside.

4 Heat a wok, then add the suet. When the suet has melted, add the steak and stir-fry for 2–3 minutes, until it is cooked but still pink in colour.

5 Pour the stock over the beef and add the tofu, mushrooms and leeks. Cook, stirring occasionally, for 4 minutes, until the leeks are tender. Divide the different ingredients equally among individual plates, spoon the stock over them and serve immediately with a few baby spinach leaves each.

> **Cook's Tip**
> Add a touch of authenticity and serve this complete meal with chopsticks and a porcelain spoon to collect the stock juices.

Ginger Pork with Black Bean Sauce

Preserved black beans provide a unique flavour in this dish. Look for them in specialist Chinese grocers.

Serves 4

350g/12oz pork fillet (tenderloin)
1 garlic clove, crushed
15ml/1 tbsp grated fresh root ginger
90ml/6 tbsp chicken stock
30ml/2 tbsp dry sherry
15ml/1 tbsp light soy sauce
5ml/1 tsp sugar

10ml/2 tsp cornflour (cornstarch)
45ml/3 tbsp groundnut (peanut) oil
2 yellow (bell) peppers, seeded and cut into strips
2 red (bell) peppers, seeded and cut into strips
1 bunch of spring onions (scallions), sliced diagonally
45ml/3 tbsp preserved black beans, coarsely chopped
fresh coriander (cilantro) sprigs, to garnish

1 Cut the pork into thin slices across the grain of the meat. Put the slices into a dish and mix them with the garlic and ginger. Cover with clear film (plastic wrap) and leave to marinate at room temperature for 15 minutes.

2 Blend together the stock, sherry, soy sauce, sugar and cornflour in a small bowl, then set the sauce mixture aside.

3 Heat the oil in a wok or large frying pan. Add the pork slices and stir-fry for 2–3 minutes. Add the yellow and red peppers and spring onions and stir-fry for a further 2 minutes.

4 Add the beans and sauce mixture and cook, stirring constantly, until thick. Serve immediately, garnished with the fresh coriander sprigs.

> **Cook's Tip**
> If you cannot find preserved black beans, use the same amount of black bean sauce instead.

Beef Energy 489kcal/2044kJ; Protein 34.7g; Carbohydrate 49g, of which sugars 6.9g; Fat 16.7g, of which saturates 6.5g; Cholesterol 68mg; Calcium 328mg; Fibre 2.4g; Sodium 916mg.
Ginger Pork Energy 302kcal/1263kJ; Protein 23.8g; Carbohydrate 22.1g, of which sugars 13.4g; Fat 12.8g, of which saturates 3.1g; Cholesterol 55mg; Calcium 41mg; Fibre 4.1g; Sodium 341mg.

Peking Beef & Pepper Stir-fry

Once the steak has marinated, this colourful dish can be prepared in just a few minutes.

Serves 4

350g/12oz rump (round) or sirloin steak, sliced into strips
30ml/2 tbsp soy sauce
30ml/2 tbsp medium sherry
15ml/1 tbsp cornflour (cornstarch)
5ml/1 tsp brown sugar
15ml/1 tbsp sunflower oil
15ml/1 tbsp sesame oil
1 garlic clove, finely chopped
15ml/1 tbsp grated fresh root ginger
1 red (bell) pepper, seeded and sliced
1 yellow (bell) pepper, seeded and sliced
115g/4oz/1 cup sugar snap peas
4 spring onions (scallions), cut into 5cm/2in pieces
30ml/2 tbsp oyster sauce
hot noodles, to serve

1 Mix together the steak strips, soy sauce, sherry, cornflour and brown sugar in a bowl. Cover with clear film (plastic wrap) and leave in a cool place to marinate for 30 minutes.

2 Heat a wok or large frying pan and add the sunflower and sesame oils. When the oils are hot add the garlic and ginger and stir-fry for about 30 seconds.

3 Add the red and yellow peppers, sugar snap peas and spring onions and stir-fry over high heat for 3 minutes.

4 Add the steak with the marinade juices to the wok or frying pan and stir-fry for a further 3–4 minutes.

5 Finally, pour in the oyster sauce and 60ml/4 tbsp water and cook, stirring constantly, until the sauce has thickened slightly. Serve immediately with hot noodles.

> **Cook's Tip**
> *Although it is made from oysters, plus other ingredients, oyster sauce will not impart a fishy flavour to the meat.*

Texan Barbecued Ribs

This barbecue or oven-roast dish of pork spare ribs cooked in a sweet and sour sauce is a favourite in the United States.

Serves 4

1.5kg/3lb (about 16) lean pork spare ribs
1 onion, finely chopped
1 large garlic clove, crushed
120ml/4fl oz/½ cup tomato purée (paste)
30ml/2 tbsp orange juice
30ml/2 tbsp red wine vinegar
5ml/1 tsp mustard
10ml/2 tsp clear honey
25g/1oz/2 tbsp soft light brown sugar
dash of Worcestershire sauce
30ml/2 tbsp vegetable oil
salt and ground black pepper
chopped fresh parsley, to garnish (optional)

1 Preheat the oven to 200°C/400°F/Gas 6. Place the pork spare ribs in a single layer in a large, shallow roasting pan and bake for 20 minutes.

2 Meanwhile, mix together the onion, garlic, tomato purée, orange juice, wine vinegar, mustard, clear honey, brown sugar, Worcestershire sauce and oil in a pan and season with salt and pepper. Bring to the boil, then lower the heat and simmer for about 5 minutes.

3 Remove the ribs from the oven and reduce the oven temperature to 180°C/350°F/Gas 4. Spoon half the sauce over the ribs, covering them well and bake for 20 minutes. Turn them over, baste with the remaining sauce and cook for 25 minutes.

4 Sprinkle the spare ribs with parsley, if using, before serving and allow three or four ribs per person.

> **Cook's Tip**
> *Use American mustard for an authentic flavour. It is sweet and mild with a very soft consistency. Otherwise, Dijon mustard, which is sharper and hotter, would work well.*

Stir-Fry Energy 225kcal/940kJ; Protein 22.7g; Carbohydrate 11.9g, of which sugars 8.9g; Fat 9.9g, of which saturates 2.4g; Cholesterol 52mg; Calcium 23mg; Fibre 3g; Sodium 713mg.
Ribs Energy 664kcal/2761kJ; Protein 56.5g; Carbohydrate 14.6g, of which sugars 14.2g; Fat 42.4g, of which saturates 13.8g; Cholesterol 199mg; Calcium 41mg; Fibre 1.1g; Sodium 258mg.

Turkish Lamb & Apricot Stew

Couscous flavoured with almonds and parsley accompanies this rich and delicious stew of lamb, apricots and chickpeas.

Serves 4

1 large aubergine
  (eggplant), diced
30ml/2 tbsp sunflower oil
1 onion, chopped
1 garlic clove, crushed
5ml/1 tsp ground cinnamon
3 cloves
450g/1lb boned leg of lamb, diced
400g/14oz can
  chopped tomatoes

115g/4oz ready-to-eat
  dried apricots
115g/4oz/1 cup canned
  chickpeas, drained and rinsed
5ml/1 tsp clear honey
salt and ground black pepper

To serve

400g/14oz/2 cups couscous,
  prepared
30ml/2 tbsp olive oil
30ml/2 tbsp chopped almonds,
  fried in a little oil
30ml/2 tbsp chopped
  fresh parsley

1 Place the diced aubergine in a colander, sprinkle with salt and leave for about 30 minutes. Heat the oil in a large flameproof casserole. Add the onion and garlic and cook, stirring occasionally, for about 5 minutes, until softened.

2 Stir in the cinnamon and cloves and cook, stirring constantly, for1 minute. Add the lamb and cook, stirring frequently, for 5–6 minutes, until evenly browned.

3 Rinse, drain and pat dry the aubergine with kitchen paper, add to the casserole and cook, stirring constantly, for 3 minutes. Add the tomatoes, 300ml/½ pint/1¼ cups water and the apricots, and season to taste with salt and pepper. Bring to the boil, then lower the heat, cover with a tight-fitting lid and simmer gently for about 45 minutes.

4 Stir the chickpeas and honey into the stew and cook for a final 15–20 minutes, or until the lamb is tender. Serve the dish accompanied by couscous with the olive oil, fried almonds and chopped parsley stirred into it.

Curried Lamb & Lentils

This colourful curry is packed with protein and low in fat, so it makes a tasty yet healthy meal.

Serves 4

8 lean boned lamb leg steaks
  (about 500g/1¼lb
  total weight)
1 onion, chopped
2 carrots, diced

1 celery stick, chopped
15ml/1 tbsp hot curry paste
30ml/2 tbsp tomato
  purée (paste)
475ml/16fl oz/2 cups chicken or
  veal stock
175g/6oz/1 cup green lentils
salt and ground black pepper
fresh coriander (cilantro) leaves,
  to garnish
boiled rice, to serve

1 Cook the lamb steaks in a large, non-stick frying pan, without any added fat, for 2–3 minutes on each side, until browned.

2 Add the onion, carrots and celery and cook, stirring occasionally, for 2 minutes, then stir in the curry paste, tomato purée, stock and lentils.

3 Bring to the boil, lower the heat, cover with a tight-fitting lid and simmer gently for 30 minutes, until tender. Add some extra stock, if necessary.

4 Season to taste with salt and pepper. Spoon the curry on to warmed plates and serve immediately, garnished with coriander and accompanied by rice.

> **Cook's Tip**
> Lentils are one of the few pulses (legumes) that do not require prolonged soaking in cold water before cooking. However, just like dried beans and peas, they should not be seasoned with salt until after cooking or their skins will become unpleasantly tough. Both green and brown lentils keep their shape well, as do the rather more expensive small Puy lentils. Red and yellow lentils are not suitable for this recipe as they tend to disintegrate during cooking.

Turkish Lamb Energy 462kcal/1931kJ; Protein 28.5g; Carbohydrate 23.2g, of which sugars 17.6g; Fat 29.1g, of which saturates 7.8g; Cholesterol 86mg; Calcium 77mg; Fibre 5.8g; Sodium 114mg.
Curried Lamb Energy 381kcal/1600kJ; Protein 35.5g; Carbohydrate 28.4g, of which sugars 4.3g; Fat 14.7g, of which saturates 6.6g; Cholesterol 95mg; Calcium 47mg; Fibre 3.2g; Sodium 144mg.

Middle-Eastern Lamb Kebabs

Skewered, grilled meats are a staple of Middle Eastern cooking. Here, marinated lamb is grilled with a colourful mix of vegetables.

Makes 4

450g/1lb boned leg of lamb, diced
75ml/5 tbsp olive oil
15ml/1 tbsp chopped fresh
  oregano or thyme, or
  10ml/2 tsp dried oregano
15ml/1 tbsp chopped
  fresh parsley
juice of ½ lemon
½ small aubergine (eggplant),
  thickly sliced and quartered
4 baby (pearl) onions, halved
2 tomatoes, quartered
4 fresh bay leaves
salt and ground black pepper
pitta bread and natural (plain)
  yogurt, to serve

1 Place the lamb in a non-metallic bowl. Mix together the olive oil, oregano or thyme, parsley and lemon juice in a jug (pitcher) and season with salt and pepper. Pour over the lamb and mix well. Cover with clear film (plastic wrap) and leave to marinate in the refrigerator for about 1 hour.

2 Preheat the grill (broiler). Thread the marinated lamb, aubergine, onions, tomatoes and bay leaves alternately on to four large skewers. (If using wooden skewers, soak them first.) Reserve the marinade.

3 Place the kebabs on a grill (broiler) rack and brush the vegetables liberally with the reserved marinade. Cook the kebabs under medium heat for 8–10 minutes on each side, basting once or twice with the juices that have collected in the bottom of the pan. Serve the kebabs immediately, accompanied by hot pitta bread and yogurt.

Cook's Tips
• For a more piquant marinade, add one or two peeled and crushed garlic cloves.
• These kebabs can also be cooked for the same length of time on a barbecue.

Mexican Spiced Roast Leg of Lamb

Make sure you push the garlic slices deeply into the meat or they will burn and develop a bitter flavour.

Serves 4
1 small leg or half leg of lamb
  (about 1.25kg/2½lb)
15ml/1 tbsp dried oregano
5ml/1 tsp ground cumin
5ml/1 tsp hot chilli powder
2 garlic cloves
45ml/3 tbsp olive oil
30ml/2 tbsp red wine vinegar
300ml/½ pint/1¼ cups chicken
  or veal stock
salt and ground black pepper
fresh oregano sprigs, to garnish

1 Preheat the oven to 220°C/425°F/Gas 7. Place the leg of lamb on a large chopping board.

2 Place the oregano, cumin and chilli powder in a bowl. Crush one of the garlic cloves and add it to the bowl. Pour in half the olive oil and mix well to form a paste.

3 Using a sharp knife, make a criss-cross pattern of fairly deep slits going through the skin and just into the meat of the leg of lamb. Press the spice paste into the slits with the back of a round-bladed knife. Peel and thinly slice the remaining garlic clove, then cut each slice in half. Push the pieces of garlic deeply into the slits made in the meat.

4 Place the lamb in a roasting pan. Mix together the vinegar and remaining oil in a bowl and pour over the meat. Season with salt and pepper.

5 Roast the lamb for about 15 minutes, then lower the oven temperature to 180°C/350°F/Gas 4 and roast for a further 1¼ hours (or a little longer if you like your meat well done).

6 Transfer the lamb to a carving board, cover with foil and leave to stand. Place the roasting pan over medium heat, pour in the stock and bring to the boil, scraping up the sediment from the base of the pan. Cook, stirring constantly, for 2–3 minutes, until slightly thickened. Carve the lamb and serve, garnished with oregano sprigs and accompanied by the gravy.

Kebabs Energy 339kcal/1409kJ; Protein 22.6g; Carbohydrate 2.7g, of which sugars 2.4g; Fat 26.5g, of which saturates 7.9g; Cholesterol 86mg; Calcium 16mg; Fibre 0.7g; Sodium 102mg.
Roast Leg Energy 733kcal/3073kJ; Protein 94.8g; Carbohydrate 4.1g, of which sugars 0.4g; Fat 37.8g, of which saturates 13.1g; Cholesterol 313mg; Calcium 27mg; Fibre 1g; Sodium 198mg.

Boeuf Bourguignon

This French classic is named after the region it comes from, Burgundy, where the local red wine is used to flavour it.

Serves 4
30ml/2 tbsp olive oil
225g/8oz piece streaky (fatty) bacon, diced
12 baby (pearl) onions
900g/2lb braising steak, cut into 5cm/2in cubes
1 large onion, thickly sliced
15g/½oz/2 tbsp plain (all-purpose) flour
about 450ml/¾ pint/scant 2 cups red Burgundy wine
1 bouquet garni
1 garlic clove
225g/8oz button (white) mushrooms, halved
salt and ground black pepper
chopped fresh parsley, to garnish

1 Heat the oil in a flameproof casserole over low heat. Add the bacon and baby onions and cook, stirring occasionally, for 7–8 minutes, until the onions are evenly browned and the bacon fat has become translucent. Remove with a slotted spoon and set aside on a plate.

2 Add the beef to the casserole, increase the heat to medium and cook, stirring frequently, until evenly browned all over. Add the sliced onion and cook, stirring occasionally for a further 4–5 minutes.

3 Sprinkle in the flour and cook, stirring constantly, for 1 minute. Gradually stir in the wine, add the bouquet garni and garlic and season with salt and pepper. Bring to the boil, then lower the heat, cover with a tight-fitting lid and simmer gently for about 2 hours.

4 Stir in the baby onions and bacon and add a little extra wine, if necessary. Add the mushrooms. Replace the lid of the casserole and cook for a further 30 minutes, or until the meat is very tender. Remove and discard the bouquet garni and garlic. Taste and adjust the seasoning, if necessary, then ladle the stew on to warmed plates, garnish with chopped fresh parsley and serve immediately.

Spiced Lamb Bake

A delicious shepherd's pie from South Africa. The recipe was originally poached from the Afrikaners' Malay slaves.

Serves 4
15ml/1 tbsp vegetable oil
1 onion, chopped
675g/1½lb minced (ground) lamb
30ml/2 tbsp medium curry paste
30ml/2 tbsp mango chutney
30ml/2 tbsp freshly squeezed lemon juice
60ml/4 tbsp chopped, blanched almonds
30ml/2 tbsp sultanas (golden raisins)
200ml/7fl oz/scant 1 cup coconut cream
2 eggs
2 bay leaves
salt and ground black pepper
broccoli florets, to serve (optional)

1 Preheat the oven to 180°C/350°F/Gas 4. Heat the oil in a large, heavy frying pan over low heat. Add the onion and cook, stirring occasionally, for 5–6 minutes, until softened but not coloured.

2 Add the minced lamb, increase the heat to medium and cook, stirring frequently to break up the lumps, for 6–8 minutes, until evenly browned.

3 Stir in the curry paste, mango chutney, lemon juice, almonds and sultanas, season well with salt and pepper and cook, stirring occasionally, for about 5 minutes.

4 Transfer the mixture to an ovenproof dish and cook in the oven, uncovered, for 10 minutes.

5 Meanwhile, beat the coconut cream with the eggs in a bowl and season with salt and pepper.

6 Remove the dish from the oven and pour the coconut custard over the meat mixture. Lay the bay leaves on the top and return the dish to the oven for 30–35 minutes, or until the top is set and golden. Spoon the bake on to warmed plates and serve immediately with cooked broccoli if you like.

Boeuf Energy 749kcal/3117kJ; Protein 63.3g; Carbohydrate 15.2g, of which sugars 8.8g; Fat 40.3g, of which saturates 14g; Cholesterol 167mg; Calcium 69mg; Fibre 2.8g; Sodium 868mg.
Lamb Energy 657kcal/2732kJ; Protein 40.1g; Carbohydrate 12.5g, of which sugars 11.7g; Fat 50.1g, of which saturates 23.4g; Cholesterol 225mg; Calcium 94mg; Fibre 1.6g; Sodium 243mg.

Greek Pasta Bake

Another excellent main meal (called *pastitsio* in Greece), this recipe is both economical and filling.

Serves 4
15ml/1 tbsp olive oil
450g/1lb minced (ground) lamb
1 onion, chopped
2 garlic cloves, crushed
30ml/2 tbsp tomato purée (paste)

25g/1oz/¼ cup plain (all-purpose) flour
300ml/½ pint/1¼ cups lamb or chicken stock
2 large tomatoes
115g/4oz cup pasta shapes
450g/1lb tub Greek (US strained plain) yogurt
2 eggs, lightly beaten
salt and ground black pepper
green salad, to serve

1 Preheat the oven to 190°C/375°F/Gas 5. Heat the oil in a large pan over medium heat. Add the lamb and cook, stirring frequently, for 5 minutes. Add the onion and garlic and cook, stirring occasionally, or a further 5 minutes.

2 Stir in the tomato purée and flour. Cook, stirring constantly, for 1 minute, then gradually stir in the stock and season to taste with salt and pepper. Bring to the boil, then lower the heat and simmer for 20 minutes.

3 Slice the tomatoes, spoon the meat mixture into an ovenproof dish and arrange the tomatoes on top.

4 Bring a pan of salted water to the boil and cook the pasta shapes for 8–10 minutes until just tender. Drain well.

5 Mix together the pasta, yogurt and eggs in a bowl. Spoon the mixture on top of the tomatoes and bake for 1 hour. Serve immediately with a crisp green salad.

> **Cook's Tip**
> Choose open pasta shapes for this dish rather than tubes, so the sauce coats the pasta all over. Try shells, spirals or bows.

Bacon Koftas

These Middle-Eastern koftas are good for barbecues and summer grills, served with lots of fresh salad.

Serves 4
225g/8oz lean smoked back bacon, coarsely chopped
75g/3oz/1½ cups fresh wholemeal (whole-wheat) breadcrumbs

2 spring onions (scallions), chopped
15ml/1 tbsp chopped fresh parsley
finely grated rind of 1 lemon
1 egg white
pinch of paprika
ground black pepper
lemon rind and fresh parsley leaves, to garnish
rice, to serve (optional)

1 Preheat the grill (broiler). Place the bacon in a food processor with the breadcrumbs, spring onions, parsley, grated lemon rind and egg white and season with pepper. Process the mixture until it is finely chopped and is beginning to bind together. Alternatively, use a mincer (meat grinder).

2 Scrape the bacon mixture into a bowl and divide into eight even-size pieces. Shape the pieces into long ovals around eight soaked wooden or bamboo skewers.

3 Sprinkle the koftas with paprika and cook under a hot grill, turning occasionally, for 8–10 minutes, until evenly browned all over and cooked through. Alternatively, cook them on a barbecue in the same way. Garnish with lemon rind and parsley leaves, then serve hot with cooked rice, if you like.

> **Cook's Tips**
> • This is a good way to spread a little meat a long way as each portion requires only 50g/2oz bacon. Use good quality bacon, preferably dry cured, for this recipe.
> • Bacon is a very useful stand-by, as it will keep for up to 3 weeks if stored in the coolest part of the refrigerator. If you buy pre-packed bacon, take note of the "use by" date printed on the packaging.

Pasta Energy 555kcal/2321kJ; Protein 36.9g; Carbohydrate 33g, of which sugars 7.5g; Fat 32.8g, of which saturates 14.1g; Cholesterol 182mg; Calcium 230mg; Fibre 2.2g; Sodium 219mg.
Koftas Energy 194kcal/813kJ; Protein 13g; Carbohydrate 14.7g, of which sugars 0.6g; Fat 9.7g, of which saturates 3.5g; Cholesterol 30mg; Calcium 30mg; Fibre 0.5g; Sodium 1040mg.

Coffee Jellies with Amaretti Cream

This impressive dessert is very easy to prepare. For the best results, use a high-roasted Arabica bean for the coffee.

For the amaretti cream
150ml/¼ pint/⅔ cup double (heavy) cream
15ml/1 tbsp icing (confectioners') sugar, sifted
10–15ml/2–3 tsp instant coffee granules dissolved in 15ml/1 tbsp hot water
6 large amaretti, crushed

Serves 4
75g/3oz/generous ⅓ cup caster (superfine) sugar
450ml/¾ pint/1¾ cups hot strong coffee
30–45ml/2–3 tbsp dark rum or coffee liqueur
20ml/4 tsp powdered gelatine

1 Put the sugar in a pan with 75ml/5 tbsp water and stir over low heat until the sugar has dissolved. Increase the heat and boil the syrup steadily, without stirring, for about 3–4 minutes.

2 Stir the hot coffee and rum or coffee liqueur into the syrup, then sprinkle the gelatine over the top and stir the mixture until it is completely dissolved.

3 Carefully pour the coffee jelly mixture into four wetted 150ml/¼ pint/⅔ cup moulds, allow to cool and then leave in the refrigerator for several hours until set.

4 To make the amaretti cream, lightly whip the cream with the icing sugar until the mixture holds stiff peaks. Stir in the dissolved coffee, then gently fold in all but 30ml/2 tbsp of the crushed amaretti.

5 To turn out, first quickly dip the moulds in hot water, then place an individual plate on the top of each mould. Holding each plate and mould firmly together, invert them.

6 Spoon a little of the amaretti cream beside each jelly. Dust over the reserved amaretti crumbs and serve immediately.

Chocolate Date Torte

Originally from Austria, this wonderful cake is delightfully rich and gooey.

175g/6oz/1½ cups walnuts or pecan nuts, chopped
5ml/2 tsp vanilla extract, plus a few extra drops

Serves 8
4 egg whites
115g/4oz/generous ⅔ cup caster (superfine) sugar
200g/7oz plain (semisweet) chocolate
175g/6oz Medjool dates, stoned (pitted) and chopped

For the frosting
200g/7oz/scant 1 cup fromage frais
200g/7oz/scant 1 cup mascarpone
icing (confectioners') sugar, to taste

1 Preheat the oven to 180°C/350°F/Gas 4. Lightly grease and base-line a 20cm/8in springform cake tin (pan).

2 To make the frosting, mix together the fromage frais and mascarpone, and a few drops of vanilla extract and icing sugar to taste, then set aside.

3 Whisk the egg whites in a clean, grease-free bowl until stiff peaks form. Whisk in 30ml/2 tbsp of the caster sugar until the meringue is thick and glossy, then fold in the remainder.

4 Chop 175g/6oz of the chocolate. Carefully fold into the meringue with the dates, nuts and 5ml/1 tsp vanilla extract. Pour into the prepared tin, level the surface and bake for about 45 minutes, until risen around the edges.

5 Allow the torte to cool in the tin for about 10 minutes, then turn out on to a wire rack. Peel off the lining paper and leave until completely cold. When cool, swirl the frosting over the top of the torte.

6 Melt the remaining chocolate in a bowl set over hot water. Spoon into a small paper piping (icing) bag, snip off the top and drizzle the chocolate over the torte. Chill in the refrigerator before serving, cut into wedges.

Jellies Energy 355kcal/1480kJ; Protein 5.5g; Carbohydrate 32.1g, of which sugars 27.7g; Fat 21.5g, of which saturates 13.1g; Cholesterol 51mg; Calcium 43mg; Fibre 0.2g; Sodium 43mg.
Torte Energy 427kcal/1784kJ; Protein 9.2g; Carbohydrate 41.5g, of which sugars 40.9g; Fat 26g, of which saturates 7.8g; Cholesterol 12mg; Calcium 57mg; Fibre 2.1g; Sodium 41mg.

Crème Caramel

This creamy, caramel-flavoured custard from France is popular worldwide.

Serves 4–6

115g/4oz/generous ½ cup granulated (white) sugar
300ml/½ pint/1¼ cups milk
300ml/½ pint/1¼ cups single (light) cream
6 eggs
75g/3oz/generous ¼ cup caster (superfine) sugar
2.5ml/½ tsp vanilla extract

1 Preheat the oven to 150°C/300°F/Gas 2 and half-fill a large roasting pan with water.

2 Place the granulated sugar in a pan with 60ml/4 tbsp water and heat gently, swirling the pan occasionally, until the sugar has dissolved. Increase the heat and boil for a good caramel colour. Immediately pour the caramel into an ovenproof soufflé dish. Place in the roasting pan and set aside.

3 To make the egg custard, heat the milk and cream together in a pan until almost boiling. Meanwhile, beat the eggs, caster sugar and vanilla extract together in a mixing bowl using a large balloon whisk.

4 Whisk the hot milk into the eggs and sugar, then strain the liquid through a sieve (strainer) into the soufflé dish, on top of the cooled caramel base.

5 Transfer the tin to the centre of the oven and bake for about 1½–2 hours (topping up the water level after 1 hour), or until the custard has set in the centre. Lift the dish carefully out of the water and leave to cool, then cover and chill overnight.

6 Run a knife around the edge of the chilled custard, then place an inverted plate (large enough to hold the caramel sauce that will flow out as well) on top of the dish. Holding the dish and plate together, turn upside down. Give both plate and dish a gentle but firm shake to loosen the crème caramel, then lift off the mould. Serve immediately.

Australian Hazelnut Pavlova

A hazelnut meringue base is topped with orange cream, nectarines and raspberries in this famous dessert.

Serves 4–6

3 egg whites
175g/6oz/1 cup caster (superfine) sugar
5ml/1 tsp cornflour (cornstarch)
5ml/1 tsp white wine vinegar
40g/1½ oz/generous ¼ cup chopped roasted hazelnuts
250ml/8fl oz/1 cup double (heavy) cream
15ml/1 tbsp orange juice
30ml/2 tbsp natural (plain) thick and creamy yogurt
2 ripe nectarines, stoned (pitted) and sliced
225g/8oz/2 cups raspberries, halved
15–30ml/1–2 tbsp redcurrant jelly, warmed

1 Preheat the oven to 140°C/275°F/Gas 1. Lightly grease a baking sheet. Draw a 20cm/8in circle on a sheet of baking parchment. Place pencil-side down on the baking sheet.

2 Place the egg whites in a clean, grease-free bowl and whisk until stiff peaks form. Whisk in the caster sugar 15g/½oz/1 tbsp at a time, whisking well after each addition.

3 Add the cornflour, vinegar and hazelnuts and fold in carefully with a large metal spoon.

4 Spoon the meringue on to the marked circle and spread out to the edges, making a dip in the centre. Bake for about 1¼–1½ hours, until crisp. Cool completely; transfer to a serving platter.

5 Whip the double cream and orange juice until the mixture is just thick, stir in the yogurt and spoon on to the meringue. Top with the prepared fruit and drizzle over the warmed redcurrant jelly. Serve immediately.

Variation
For extra colour, add a couple of peeled and sliced kiwi fruit.

Caramel Energy 318kcal/1335kJ; Protein 9.8g; Carbohydrate 36.6g, of which sugars 36.6g; Fat 16g, of which saturates 8.2g; Cholesterol 221mg; Calcium 150mg; Fibre 0g; Sodium 108mg.
Pavlova Energy 427kcal/1783kJ; Protein 5g; Carbohydrate 44.1g, of which sugars 43.2g; Fat 26.9g, of which saturates 14.3g; Cholesterol 57mg; Calcium 71mg; Fibre 2.2g; Sodium 50mg.

Apricot & Almond Jalousie

Jalousie means "shutter", and the slatted pastry topping of this pie looks exactly like French window shutters. The dish not only looks attractive, but tastes wonderful, too.

Serves 4
225g/8oz ready-made puff pastry
a little beaten egg
90ml/6 tbsp apricot conserve
25g/1oz/2 tbsp caster (superfine) sugar
30ml/2 tbsp flaked almonds
cream, to serve

1 Preheat the oven to 220°C/425°F/Gas 7. Roll out the pastry on a lightly floured surface and cut into a square measuring 30cm/12in. Cut in half to make two rectangles.

2 Place one piece of pastry on a wetted baking sheet and brush all round the edges with beaten egg. Spread the apricot conserve over the unbrushed part of the rectangle.

3 Fold the remaining rectangle in half lengthways and cut about eight diagonal slits from the centre fold to within about 1cm/½in from the edge all the way along.

4 Unfold the cut pastry and lay it on top of the pastry on the baking sheet. Press the pastry edges together well to seal and knock them up with the back of a knife.

5 Brush the slashed pastry with water and sprinkle over the caster sugar and flaked almonds.

6 Bake in the oven for 25–30 minutes, until well risen and golden brown. Remove the jalousie from the oven and leave to cool. Serve sliced, accompanied by cream.

Chocolate Eclairs

These choux pastry éclairs are filled with a luscious vanilla-flavoured cream.

Serves 12
300ml/½ pint/1¼ cups double (heavy) cream
10ml/2 tsp icing (confectioners') sugar, sifted
1.5ml/¼ tsp vanilla extract

115g/4oz plain (semisweet) chocolate
25g/1oz/2 tbsp butter

For the pastry
65g/2½oz/9 tbsp plain (all-purpose) flour
pinch of salt
50g/2oz/¼ cup butter, diced
2 eggs, lightly beaten

1 Preheat the oven to 200°C/400°F/Gas 6. Grease a large baking sheet and line with baking parchment.

2 To make the pastry, sift the flour and salt on to a small sheet of baking parchment. Very gently heat the butter and 150ml/¼ pint/⅔ cup water in a pan until the butter has melted. Bring to a rolling boil, then remove from the heat and immediately tip in all the flour. Beat vigorously to mix well. Return the pan to a low heat. Beat the mixture until it leaves the sides of the pan and forms a ball. Set aside and allow to cool for 2–3 minutes.

3 Beat in the eggs, a little at a time, to form a smooth, shiny paste. Spoon into a piping (pastry) bag fitted with a 2.5cm/1in plain nozzle. Pipe 10cm/4in lengths on to the baking sheet.

4 Bake for 25–30 minutes, or until the pastries are well risen and golden brown. Make a neat slit along the side of each to release the steam. Lower the temperature to 180°C/350°F/Gas 4 and bake for a further 5 minutes. Cool on a wire rack.

5 To make the filling, whip the cream with the icing sugar and vanilla until it just holds its shape. Pipe into the éclairs.

6 Place the chocolate and 30ml/2 tbsp water in a small bowl set over a pan of hot water. Melt, stirring, then remove from the heat and gradually stir in the butter. Use the chocolate mixture to coat the éclairs. Place on a wire rack and leave to set.

<table>
<tr><td colspan="2">

Cook's Tip
Make smaller individual jalousies and serve them with morning coffee, if you like. Use other flavours of fruit conserve to ring the changes – a summer berry conserve would be delicious.

</td></tr>
</table>

Eclairs Energy 253Kcal/1046kJ; Protein 2.7g; Carbohydrate 10.8g, of which sugars 6.5g; Fat 22.4g, of which saturates 13.5g; Cholesterol 86mg; Calcium 30mg; Fibre 0.4g; Sodium 58mg.
Jalousie Energy 339kcal/1423kJ; Protein 4.9g; Carbohydrate 43.5g, of which sugars 23.2g; Fat 18g, of which saturates 0.3g; Cholesterol 0mg; Calcium 56mg; Fibre 0.6g; Sodium 186mg.

Baked American Cheesecake

The lemon-flavoured cream cheese provides a subtle filling for this classic dessert.

Makes 9 squares
175g/6oz/1½ cups crushed digestive biscuits (graham crackers)
40g/1½ oz/3 tbsp butter, melted, plus extra for greasing

For the topping
450g/1lb/2½ cups curd (farmer's) cheese or full-fat soft (cream) cheese

115g/4oz/generous ½ cup caster (superfine) sugar
3 eggs
finely grated rind of 1 lemon
15ml/1 tbsp lemon juice
2.5ml/½ tsp vanilla extract
15ml/1 tbsp cornflour (cornstarch)
30ml/2 tbsp sour cream
150ml/¼ pint/⅔ cup sour cream and 1.5ml/¼ tsp ground cinnamon, to decorate

1 Preheat the oven to 170°C/325°F/Gas 3. Lightly grease an 18cm/7in square loose-based cake tin (pan), then line the base with baking parchment.

2 Place the crushed biscuits and butter in a bowl and mix well. Turn into the base of the prepared cake tin and press down firmly with a potato masher.

3 To make the topping, place the curd or soft cheese in a mixing bowl, add the sugar and beat well until smooth. Add the eggs one at a time, beating well after each addition.

4 Stir in the lemon rind and juice, the vanilla extract, cornflour and 30ml/2 tbsp sour cream. Beat until the mixture is smooth. Pour the mixture on to the biscuit base and level the surface.

5 Bake for 1¼ hours, or until the cheesecake has set in the centre. Turn off the oven but leave the cheesecake inside until completely cold.

6 Remove the cheesecake from the tin, top with the sour cream and swirl with the back of a spoon. Sprinkle with cinnamon and serve cut into squares.

Mango Ice Cream

Canned mangoes are used to make a deliciously rich and creamy ice cream, with a delicate oriental flavour.

Serves 4–6
2 x 425g/15oz cans sliced mango, drained

50g/2oz/¼ cup caster (superfine) sugar
30ml/2 tbsp lime juice
45ml/3 tbsp hot water
15ml/1 tbsp powdered gelatine
350ml/12fl oz/1½ cups double (heavy) cream, lightly whipped
fresh mint sprigs, to decorate

1 Reserve four slices of mango for decoration and chop the remainder. Place the chopped mango pieces in a bowl with the caster sugar and lime juice.

2 Put the hot water in a small heatproof bowl and sprinkle over the gelatine. Place the bowl over a pan of gently simmering water and stir until the gelatine has dissolved. Pour on to the mango mixture and mix well.

3 Add the lightly whipped cream and fold into the mango mixture. Pour the mixture into a plastic freezer container and freeze until half frozen.

4 Place the half-frozen ice cream in a food processor or blender and process until smooth. Spoon back into the container and return to the freezer to freeze completely.

5 Remove from the freezer 10 minutes before serving and place in the refrigerator. Serve scoops of ice cream decorated with pieces of the reserved sliced mango and fresh mint sprigs.

Cook's Tip
• Transferring the ice cream to the refrigerator for a short time before serving allows it to soften slightly, making scooping easier and helping the flavour to be more pronounced.
• Use a metal scoop to serve the ice cream, dipping the scoop briefly in warm water between servings. Or simply slice, if easier.

Cheesecake Energy 311kcal/1302kJ; Protein 11.4g; Carbohydrate 30.8g, of which sugars 18.5g; Fat 17.4g, of which saturates 9.7g; Cholesterol 105mg; Calcium 112mg; Fibre 0.4g; Sodium 396mg.
Ice Cream Energy 409kcal/1701kJ; Protein 1.4g; Carbohydrate 32.4g, of which sugars 32.3g; Fat 31.3g, of which saturates 19.5g; Cholesterol 80mg; Calcium 44mg; Fibre 0.9g; Sodium 17mg.

Pecan Cake

This delicious cake is an example of the French influence on Mexican cooking. Serve with a few redcurrants for a splash of uplifting colour.

Serves 8–10

115g/4oz/1 cup pecan nuts
115g/4oz/½ cup butter, softened
115g/4oz/½ cup soft light brown sugar
5ml/1 tsp vanilla extract
4 large eggs, separated
75g/3oz/⅔ cup plain (all-purpose) flour
pinch of salt
12 whole pecan nuts, to decorate
whipped cream or crème fraîche, to serve

For drizzling

50g/2oz/¼ cup butter
120ml/4fl oz/scant ½ cup clear honey

1 Preheat the oven to 180°C/350°F/Gas 4. Grease a 20cm/8in round cake tin (pan). Toast the nuts in a dry frying pan for 5 minutes, shaking frequently. Grind finely and place in a bowl.

2 Cream the butter with the sugar in a mixing bowl, then beat in the vanilla extract and egg yolks.

3 Add the flour to the ground nuts and mix well. Whisk the egg whites with the salt in a clean, grease-free bowl until soft peaks form. Fold the whites into the butter mixture, then gently fold in the flour and nut mixture.

4 Spoon the mixture into the cake tin and bake for 30 minutes or until a skewer inserted in the centre comes out clean.

5 Cool the cake in the tin for 5 minutes, then remove the sides of the tin. Stand the cake on a wire rack until cold.

6 Remove the cake from the base of the tin if necessary, then return it to the rack and arrange the pecans on top. Transfer to a plate. Melt the butter for drizzling in a small pan, add the honey and bring to the boil, stirring. Lower the heat and simmer for 3 minutes, then pour over the cake. Serve with whipped cream or crème fraîche.

Chilled Chocolate Slice

This is a very rich family pudding, but it is also designed to use up the occasional leftover.

Serves 6–8

115g/4oz/½ cup butter, melted
225g/8oz ginger nut biscuits (gingersnaps), finely crushed
50g/2oz stale sponge cake crumbs
60–75ml/4–5 tbsp orange juice
115g/4oz stoned (pitted) dates
25g/1oz/¼ cup finely chopped nuts
175g/6oz dark (bittersweet) chocolate
300ml/½ pint/1¼ cups whipping cream
grated chocolate and icing (confectioners') sugar, to decorate

1 Mix together the butter and ginger nut biscuit crumbs, then pack around the sides and base of an 18cm/7in loose-based flan tin (pan). Chill while making the filling.

2 Put the cake crumbs into a large bowl with the orange juice and leave to soak. Warm the dates thoroughly, then mash and blend into the cake crumbs along with the nuts.

3 Melt the chocolate with 45–60ml/3–4 tbsp of the cream. Softly whip the rest of the cream, then fold in the melted chocolate mixture.

4 Stir the cream and chocolate mixture into the crumbs and mix well. Pour into the prepared tin, mark into portions with a sharp knife and leave to set.

5 Scatter the grated chocolate over the top and dust with icing sugar. Serve cut into wedges.

> **Cook's Tip**
> This dessert is delicious served with slices of fresh fruit, such as peaches, mango or pineapple. Alternatively, offer plums or nectarines poached in a little wine and sugar, or try orange segments in a syrup made from sugar, water and orange juice.

Pecan Cake Energy 428Kcal/1785kJ; Protein 6.2g; Carbohydrate 34.7g, of which sugars 27.4g; Fat 30.5g, of which saturates 12.5g; Cholesterol 158mg; Calcium 51mg; Fibre 1g; Sodium 170mg.
Chocolate Slice Energy 545kcal/2269kJ; Protein 4.8g; Carbohydrate 45.8g, of which sugars 32g; Fat 39.3g, of which saturates 22.6g; Cholesterol 85mg; Calcium 80mg; Fibre 1.4g; Sodium 198mg.

Tangerine Trifle

An unusual variation on a traditional English dish – of course, you can add a little alcohol if you wish.

Serves 4
5 trifle sponges, halved
  lengthways
30ml/2 tbsp apricot jam
15–20 ratafia biscuits (almond
  macaroons)

142g/4³⁄₄oz packet tangerine jelly
  (gelatine)
300g/11oz can mandarin
  oranges, drained, reserving juice
600ml/1 pint/2¹⁄₂ cups ready-
  made custard
whipped cream and shreds of
  orange rind, to decorate
caster (superfine) sugar, for
  sprinkling

1 Spread the halved sponge cakes with apricot jam and arrange in the base of a deep serving bowl or glass dish. Sprinkle the ratafias over the top.

2 Break up the jelly into a heatproof measuring jug (cup), add the juice from the canned mandarins and dissolve in a pan of hot water or in the microwave. Stir until the liquid is clear.

3 Make up to 600ml/1 pint/2¹⁄₂ cups with ice-cold water, stir well and leave to cool for up to 30 minutes. Scatter the mandarin oranges over the cake and ratafias.

4 Pour the jelly over the mandarin oranges, cake and ratafias and chill for 1 hour or more.

5 When the jelly has set, pour the custard over the top and chill again in the refrigerator.

6 When ready to serve, pipe the whipped cream over the custard. Wash the orange rind shreds, sprinkle them with caster sugar and use to decorate the trifle.

> **Cook's Tip**
> For an even better flavour, why not make your own custard?

Blackberry & Apple Romanoff

The unbeatable combination of blackberries and apples gives this Russian dessert a delicious flavour. Surprisingly easy to make, the dish offers a stunning finale to a meal.

Serves 6–8
350g/12oz sharp eating apples,
  peeled, cored and chopped
40g/1¹⁄₂oz/3 tbsp caster
  (superfine) sugar

250ml/8fl oz/1 cup whipping
  cream
5ml/1 tsp grated lemon rind
90ml/6 tbsp Greek (US strained
  plain) yogurt
50g/2oz (about 4–6) crisp
  meringues, roughly crumbled
225g/8oz/2 cups blackberries
  (fresh or frozen)
whipped cream, a few
  blackberries and fresh mint
  leaves, to decorate

1 Line a 900ml–1.2 litre/1¹⁄₂–2 pint/4–5 cup round, deep freezerproof bowl with clear film (plastic wrap). Toss the chopped apples into a pan with 1oz/2 tbsp sugar and cook for 2–3 minutes until softened. Mash with a fork and leave to cool.

2 Whip the cream and fold in the lemon rind, yogurt, the remaining sugar, the mashed apples and the meringues.

3 Gently stir in the blackberries, then turn the mixture into the prepared bowl and freeze for 1–3 hours.

4 Loosen the edges with a knife, then turn out on to a plate and remove the clear film. Decorate with whirls of whipped cream, blackberries and mint leaves.

> **Cook's Tip**
> If you would prefer a more fruity decoration, try serving with a blackberry sauce. Put 225g/8oz blackberries in a pan with a little sugar and cook over low heat for about 5 minutes until just soft. Press half through a sieve (strainer), then mix the purée with the rest of the berries. Cool. Add a splash of crème de cassis liqueur, if you wish. Spoon a little over the dessert and serve the rest as an accompanying sauce.

Trifle Energy 566kcal/2392kJ; Protein 12.9g; Carbohydrate 106.7g, of which sugars 74.2g; Fat 11g, of which saturates 3.2g; Cholesterol 116mg; Calcium 244mg; Fibre 1.4g; Sodium 240mg.
Romanoff Energy 198kcal/825kJ; Protein 2.1g; Carbohydrate 17.6g, of which sugars 17.6g; Fat 13.8g, of which saturates 8.5g; Cholesterol 33mg; Calcium 52mg; Fibre 1.6g; Sodium 25mg.

Pear & Blackberry Brown Betty

This old English recipe is very easy to make. The delicious fruity pudding simply consists of layers of golden breadcrumbs and fresh fruit. Just the thing for feeding family and friends, it is lovely served with hot home-made custard, pouring cream or ice cream.

Serves 4–6
75g/3oz/6 tbsp butter, diced, plus extra for greasing
175g/6oz/3 cups fresh breadcrumbs
450g/1lb ripe pears
450g/1lb/4 cups blackberries
grated rind and juice of 1 small orange
115g/4oz/1/2 cup demerara (raw) sugar, plus extra for sprinkling

1 Preheat the oven to 180°C/350°F/Gas 4. Heat the butter in a heavy frying pan over medium heat and add the fresh breadcrumbs. Stir until golden, then remove from the heat.

2 Peel and core the pears, then cut them into thick slices and mix with the blackberries, orange rind and juice.

3 Mix the demerara sugar with the breadcrumbs, then layer with the fruit in a 900ml/1 1/2 pint/3¾ cup buttered baking dish, beginning and ending with a layer of sugared breadcrumbs.

4 Sprinkle the extra demerara sugar over the top. Cover the baking dish, then bake the pudding for 20 minutes.

5 Uncover the pudding, then bake for a further 30–35 minutes, until the fruit is cooked and the top is brown and crisp.

> **Cook's Tip**
> This is a great way to use up slightly stale bread; just process the crustless bread in a blender or food processor to form crumbs. Flavour the breadcrumbs with a little ground cinnamon and grated nutmeg for a touch of added spice.

Queen of Puddings

This great hot pudding was developed from a seventeenth-century recipe by Queen Victoria's chefs at Buckingham Palace.

Serves 4
75g/3oz/1 1/2 cups fresh breadcrumbs

50g/2oz/1/4 cup caster (superfine) sugar, plus about 5ml/1 tsp for sprinkling
5ml/1 tsp grated lemon rind
600ml/1 pint/2 1/2 cups milk
4 eggs
butter, for greasing
45ml/3 tbsp raspberry jam, warmed

1 Stir the breadcrumbs, 25g/1oz/2 tbsp of the sugar and the lemon rind together in a heatproof bowl. Bring the milk to the boil in a pan, then stir into the breadcrumbs.

2 Separate three of the eggs and beat the yolks with the whole egg. Stir into the breadcrumb mixture, pour into a buttered baking dish and leave to stand for 30 minutes. Meanwhile, preheat the oven to 160°C/325°F/Gas 3. Bake the pudding for 50–60 minutes, until set.

3 Whisk the egg whites in a large, clean grease-free bowl until stiff but not dry, then gradually whisk in 25g/1oz/2 tbsp caster sugar until the mixture is thick and glossy, taking care not to overwhisk.

4 Spread the raspberry jam over the set pudding, then spoon over the meringue to cover the top completely.

5 Evenly sprinkle about 5ml/1tsp sugar over the meringue, then bake for a further 15 minutes, until the meringue is beginning to turn a light golden colour.

> **Variation**
> Ring the changes by using another flavoured jam or a layer of fruit purée – poach the fruit with a little sugar and water, then purée in a blender or food processor and strain, if necessary.

Queen Energy 293kcal/1238kJ; Protein 13.7g; Carbohydrate 43.7g, of which sugars 29.7g; Fat 8.5g, of which saturates 3.2g; Cholesterol 199mg; Calcium 242mg; Fibre 0.4g; Sodium 281mg.
Brown Betty Energy 324kcal/1362kJ; Protein 4.5g; Carbohydrate 54.8g, of which sugars 32.9g; Fat 11.1g, of which saturates 6.5g; Cholesterol 27mg; Calcium 90mg; Fibre 4.6g; Sodium 303mg.

Baked Stuffed Apples

When apples are plentiful, this traditional Middle-Eastern pudding is a popular and easy choice. The filling of dried apricots, honey and ground almonds gives a new twist to an old favourite.

Serves 4
75g/3oz/scant 1 cup ground almonds
25g/1oz/2 tbsp butter, softened
5ml/1 tsp clear honey
1 egg yolk
50g/2oz dried apricots, chopped
4 cooking apples, preferably Bramleys

1 Preheat the oven to 200°C/400°F/Gas 6. Beat together the almonds, butter, honey, egg yolk and apricots.

2 Stamp out the cores from the cooking apples using a large apple corer, then score a line with the point of a sharp knife around the circumference of each apple.

3 Lightly grease a shallow baking dish, then arrange the cooking apples in the dish.

4 Using a small spoon, divide the apricot mixture among the cavities in the apples, then bake in the oven for 45–60 minutes, until the apples are fluffy.

> **Cook's Tip**
> Scoring the apples around the middle helps to prevent them from bursting during cooking.

> **Variations**
> To ring the changes, replace the dried apricots with seedless raisins or sultanas (golden raisins). Alternatively, fill the cored apples with chopped dates, mixed with finely chopped walnuts and little soft light brown sugar, then top each with a knob (pat) of butter and bake as above.

Kentish Cherry Batter Pudding

Kent, known as the "Garden of England", is particularly well known for cherries and the dishes made from them. This method of baking the fruit in batter is an absolute winner.

Serves 4
45ml/3 tbsp Kirsch (optional)
450g/1lb dark cherries, pitted
50g/2oz/½ cup plain (all-purpose) flour
50g/2oz/¼ cup caster (superfine) sugar
2 eggs, separated
300ml/½ pint/1¼ cups milk
75g/3oz/6 tbsp butter, melted
caster (superfine) sugar, for sprinkling

1 Sprinkle the Kirsch, if using, over the cherries in a small bowl and leave them to soak for about 30 minutes.

2 Mix the flour and sugar together, then slowly stir in the egg yolks and milk to make a smooth batter. Stir in half the butter and set aside for 30 minutes.

3 Preheat the oven to 220°C/425°F/Gas 7, then pour the remaining butter into a 600ml/1 pint/2½ cup baking dish and put in the oven to heat.

4 Whisk the egg whites until stiff peaks form, then fold into the batter with the cherries and Kirsch, if using. Pour into the dish and bake for 15 minutes.

5 Reduce the oven temperature to 180°C/350°F/Gas 4 and bake for 20 minutes, or until golden and set in the centre. Serve sprinkled with sugar.

> **Cook's Tip**
> It is worth the effort of pitting the cherries as it makes the dish easier to eat. Use a cherry stoner (pitter) or slit each fruit with the point of a small sharp knife and prise out the stones (pits).

Baked Apples Energy 237kcal/989kJ; Protein 5.5g; Carbohydrate 16.3g, of which sugars 15.8g; Fat 17.2g, of which saturates 4.5g; Cholesterol 64mg; Calcium 65mg; Fibre 3.8g; Sodium 47mg.
Pudding Energy 357kcal/1493kJ; Protein 8g; Carbohydrate 39.4g, of which sugars 29.8g; Fat 19.8g, of which saturates 11.4g; Cholesterol 140mg; Calcium 147mg; Fibre 1.4g; Sodium 183mg.

Zabaglione

A much-loved simple Italian dessert traditionally made with Marsala, an Italian fortified wine.

Serves 4
4 egg yolks
50g/2oz/¼ cup (superfine) sugar
60ml/4 tbsp Marsala
amaretti, to serve

1 Half fill a medium pan with water and bring to a simmer.

2 Place the egg yolks and caster sugar in a large heatproof bowl and whisk with an electric whisk until the mixture turns pale yellow and thick.

3 Gradually add the Marsala, about 15ml/1 tbsp at a time, whisking well after each addition (at this stage the mixture will be quite runny).

4 Place the bowl over the pan of gently simmering water and continue to whisk for at least 5–7 minutes, until the mixture becomes thick and mousse-like; when the beaters are lifted they should leave a thick trail on the surface of the mixture. (If you don't beat the mixture for long enough, the zabaglione will be too runny and will probably separate.)

5 Pour into four warmed stemmed glasses and serve immediately with the amaretti for dipping.

Cook's Tip
If you don't have any Marsala, substitute Madeira, a medium-sweet sherry or a dessert wine.

Variation
For chocolate zabaglione, whisk in 20ml/4 tsp unsweetened cocoa powder with the Marsala at step 3.

Thai-fried Bananas

In this very easy dessert, bananas are simply fried in butter, sugar and lime juice.

Serves 4
40g/1½ oz/3 tbsp unsalted (sweet) butter
4 large slightly under-ripe bananas
15ml/1 tbsp desiccated (dry unsweetened shredded) coconut
50g/2oz/¼ cup soft light brown sugar
60ml/4 tbsp lime juice
2 lime slices, to decorate
thick and creamy natural (plain) yogurt, to serve

1 Heat the butter in a large frying pan or wok and fry the bananas for 1–2 minutes on each side until golden. Meanwhile, dry-fry the coconut in a small frying pan until golden; reserve.

2 Sprinkle the sugar into the pan with the bananas, add the lime juice and cook, stirring, until dissolved. Sprinkle the coconut over the bananas, decorate with lime and serve with yogurt.

Hot Spiced Bananas

Bananas baked in a rum and fruit syrup are perfect for impromptu entertaining.

Serves 6
6 ripe bananas
butter, for greasing
200g/7oz/1 cup light muscovado (brown) sugar
250ml/8fl oz/1 cup unsweetened pineapple juice
120ml/4fl oz/½ cup dark rum
2 cinnamon sticks
12 whole cloves

1 Preheat the oven to 180°C/350°F/Gas 4. Cut the bananas, at a slant, into 2.5cm/1in pieces. Arrange in a greased baking dish.

2 Mix the sugar and pineapple juice in a pan. Heat gently until the sugar has dissolved, stirring occasionally. Add the rum, cinnamon sticks and cloves. Bring to the boil, then remove from the heat. Pour over the bananas and bake for 25–30 minutes until the bananas are hot and tender.

Zabaglione Energy 134kcal/561kJ; Protein 3g; Carbohydrate 14.9g, of which sugars 14.9g; Fat 5.5g, of which saturates 1.6g; Cholesterol 202mg; Calcium 31mg; Fibre 0g; Sodium 10mg.
Thai-fried Energy 241kcal/1013kJ; Protein 1.5g; Carbohydrate 36.6g, of which sugars 34.3g; Fat 10.9g, of which saturates 7.3g; Cholesterol 21mg; Calcium 15mg; Fibre 1.6g; Sodium 64mg.
Hot Spiced Energy 288kcal/1221kJ; Protein 1.5g; Carbohydrate 62.4g, of which sugars 60.1g; Fat 0.3g, of which saturates 0.1g; Cholesterol 0mg; Calcium 27mg; Fibre 1.1g; Sodium 6mg.

Crêpes Suzette

This dish is a classic of French cuisine and still enjoys worldwide popularity.

Makes 8

115g/4oz/1 cup plain (all-purpose) flour
pinch of salt
1 egg
1 egg yolk
300ml/½ pint/1¼ cups semi-skimmed milk

15g/½ oz/1 tbsp butter, melted, plus extra, for shallow frying

For the sauce

2 large oranges
50g/2oz/¼ cup butter
50g/2oz/¼ cup soft light brown sugar
15ml/1 tbsp Grand Marnier
15ml/1 tbsp brandy

1 Sift the flour and salt into a bowl and make a well in the centre. Crack the egg and extra yolk into the well. Stir the eggs to incorporate all the flour. When the mixture thickens, gradually pour in the milk, beating well after each addition, until a smooth batter is formed. Stir in the butter, transfer to a jug, cover and chill for 30 minutes.

2 Heat a shallow frying pan, add a little butter and melt until sizzling. Pour in a little batter, tilting the pan to cover the base. Cook over medium heat for 1–2 minutes until lightly browned underneath, then flip and cook for a further minute. Make eight crêpes and stack them on a plate.

3 Pare the rind from one of the oranges and reserve about 5ml/1 tsp. Squeeze the juice from both oranges.

4 To make the sauce, melt the butter in a large frying pan and heat the sugar with the orange rind and juice until dissolved and gently bubbling. Fold each crêpe into quarters. Add to the pan one at a time, coat in the sauce and fold in half again. Move to the side of the pan to make room for the others.

5 Pour on the Grand Marnier and brandy and cook gently for 2–3 minutes, until the sauce has slightly caramelized. Sprinkle with the reserved orange rind and serve immediately.

Bananas with Dark Rum & Raisins

A classic way of serving bananas, the rum is set alight just before serving. This gives the fruit a perfectly, irresistible Caribbean flavour.

Serves 4

40g/1½ oz/scant ¼ cup seedless raisins
75ml/5 tbsp dark rum

50g/2oz/4 tbsp unsalted (sweet) butter
50g/2oz/¼ cup soft light brown sugar
4 bananas, halved lengthways
1.5ml/¼ tsp grated nutmeg
1.5ml/¼ tsp ground cinnamon
30ml/2 tbsp slivered almonds, toasted
chilled sour cream or vanilla ice cream, to serve (optional)

1 Put the raisins in a bowl with the rum. Leave them to soak for about 30 minutes to plump up.

2 Melt the butter in a frying pan, add the sugar and stir until completely dissolved. Add the bananas and cook for a few minutes until tender.

3 Sprinkle the spices over the bananas, then pour over the soaked raisins and rum. Carefully set alight using a long taper and stir gently to mix.

4 Scatter over the slivered almonds and serve immediately with chilled sour cream or vanilla ice cream, if you wish.

> **Cook's Tips**
> • Chose almost-ripe bananas with evenly coloured skins, either all yellow or just green at the tips. Over-ripe bananas will not hold their shape as well when cooked.
> • Setting light to the rum – known as flambéeing – dispels most of the alcohol content, but gives the bananas an intense flavour. Stand well back when you set the rum alight and shake the pan gently until the flames subside.

Crêpes Energy 195kcal/818kJ; Protein 4.4g; Carbohydrate 23.8g, of which sugars 12.8g; Fat 8.9g, of which saturates 5.1g; Cholesterol 69mg; Calcium 100mg; Fibre 1.3g; Sodium 79mg.
Bananas Energy 352kcal/1474kJ; Protein 3.1g; Carbohydrate 43.8g, of which sugars 41.3g; Fat 14.8g, of which saturates 7g; Cholesterol 27mg; Calcium 38mg; Fibre 1.9g; Sodium 85mg.

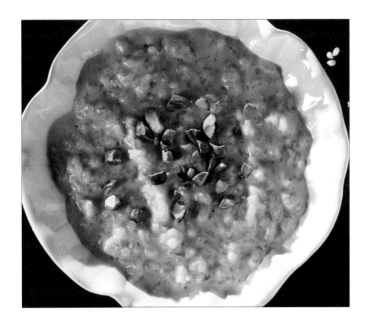

Orange Rice Pudding

In Spain, Greece, Italy and Morocco creamy rice puddings are a favourite dish, especially when sweetened with honey. This version is enhanced with a fresh orange flavour.

Serves 4
50g/2oz/¼ cup short grain pudding rice
600ml/1 pint/2½ cups milk

30–45ml/2–3 tbsp clear honey, to taste
finely grated rind of ½ small orange
150ml/¼ pint/⅔ cup double (heavy) cream
15ml/1 tbsp chopped pistachios, toasted

1 Mix the rice with the milk, honey and orange rind in a pan and bring to the boil, then reduce the heat, cover the pan with a tight-fitting lid and simmer very gently for about 1¼ hours, stirring regularly.

2 Remove the lid and continue cooking and stirring for about 15–20 minutes, until the rice is creamy.

3 Pour in the cream and simmer for 5–8 minutes longer. Serve the rice sprinkled with the chopped toasted pistachios in individual warmed bowls.

> **Cook's Tip**
> Make sure you use short grain rice for this recipe; the small chalky grains absorb liquid well, producing a creamy texture.

> **Variation**
> For a more fragrant version, omit the grated orange rind and stir in 15ml/1 tbsp orange flower water, 15ml/1 tbsp ground almonds and 5ml/1 tsp almond extract at step 3, along with the cream. Serve sprinkled with chopped dates and pistachios.

Apple & Blackberry Nut Crumble

This much-loved British dish of apples and blackberries is topped with a golden, sweet crumble. The addition of nuts gives an extra-delicious crunchy texture.

Serves 4
900g/2lb (about 4 medium) cooking apples, peeled, cored and sliced
115g/4oz/½ cup butter, diced, plus extra for greasing

115g/4oz/½ cup soft light brown sugar
175g/6oz/1½ cups blackberries
75g/3oz/¾ cup wholemeal (whole-wheat) flour
75g/3oz/¾ cup plain (all-purpose) flour
2.5ml/½ tsp ground cinnamon
45ml/3 tbsp chopped mixed nuts, toasted
custard, cream or ice cream, to serve

1 Preheat the oven to 180°C/350°F/Gas 4. Lightly butter a 1.2 litre/2 pint/5 cup ovenproof dish.

2 Place the apples in a pan with 25g/1oz/2 tbsp of the butter, 25g/1oz/2 tbsp of the sugar and 15ml/1 tbsp water. Cover with a tight-fitting lid and cook gently for about 10 minutes, until the apples are just tender but still holding their shape.

3 Remove from the heat and gently stir in the blackberries. Spoon the mixture into the ovenproof dish and set aside while you make the topping.

4 To make the crumble topping, sift the flours and cinnamon into a bowl, tipping in any of the bran left in the sieve (strainer). Add the remaining 75g/3oz/6 tbsp butter and rub into the flour with your fingertips until the mixture resembles fine breadcrumbs. Alternatively, you can use a food processor to do this stage for you.

5 Stir in the remaining sugar and the nuts and mix well. Sprinkle the crumble topping over the fruit.

6 Bake the crumble for 35–40 minutes until the top is golden brown. Serve immediately with custard, cream or ice cream.

Pudding Energy 355kcal/1477kJ; Protein 7.4g; Carbohydrate 26.6g, of which sugars 16.5g; Fat 24.8g, of which saturates 14.4g; Cholesterol 60mg; Calcium 206mg; Fibre 0.2g; Sodium 94mg.
Crumble Energy 573kcal/2398kJ; Protein 6.8g; Carbohydrate 68.3g, of which sugars 42.3g; Fat 32.2g, of which saturates 15.7g; Cholesterol 61mg; Calcium 86mg; Fibre 5.6g; Sodium 181mg.

Apple Strudel

This great Austrian dessert is traditionally made with strudel pastry, but it is just as good prepared with ready-made filo pastry.

Serves 4–6
75g/3oz/³⁄₄ cup hazelnuts, chopped and roasted
30ml/2 tbsp nibbed almonds, roasted
50g/2oz/4 tbsp demerara (raw) sugar
2.5ml/¹⁄₂ tsp ground cinnamon
grated rind and juice of ¹⁄₂ lemon
2 large cooking apples, peeled, cored and chopped
50g/2oz/¹⁄₃ cup sultanas (golden raisins)
4 large sheets filo pastry
50g/2oz/4 tbsp unsalted (sweet) butter, melted
sifted icing (confectioners') sugar, for dusting
cream, custard or yogurt, to serve

1 Preheat the oven to 190°C/375°F/Gas 5. In a bowl mix together the hazelnuts, almonds, sugar, cinnamon, lemon rind and juice, apples and sultanas. Set aside.

2 Lay one sheet of filo pastry on a clean dish towel and brush with melted butter. Lay a second sheet on top and brush again with melted butter. Repeat with the remaining two sheets.

3 Spread the fruit and nut mixture over the pastry, leaving a 7.5cm/3in border at each of the shorter ends. Fold the pastry ends in over the filling. Roll up from one long edge to the other, using the dish towel to help.

4 Carefully transfer the strudel to a greased baking sheet, placing it seam-side down. Brush all over with butter and bake for 30–35 minutes until golden and crisp. Dust the strudel generously with icing sugar and serve while still hot with cream, custard or yogurt.

Cook's Tip
Chilled filo pastry sheets are available from most supermarkets. Work quickly with the thin sheets as they dry out rapidly.

Banana, Maple & Lime Crêpes

Crêpes are a treat any day of the week, and they can be made in advance and stored in the freezer for convenience.

Serves 4
115g/4oz/1 cup plain (all-purpose) flour
1 egg white
250ml/8fl oz/1 cup skimmed milk
sunflower oil, for frying

For the filling
4 bananas, sliced
45ml/3 tbsp maple or golden (light corn) syrup
30ml/2 tbsp freshly squeezed lime juice
strips of lime rind, to decorate

1 Beat together the flour, egg white, milk and 50ml/2f oz/¹⁄₄ cup water until the mixture is smooth and bubbly. Chill in the refrigerator until ready to use.

2 Heat a small amount of oil in a non-stick frying pan and pour in enough batter just to coat the base. Swirl it around the pan to coat evenly.

3 Cook until golden, then toss or turn and cook the other side. Place on a plate, cover with foil and keep hot while making the remaining pancakes.

4 To make the filling, place the bananas, syrup and lime juice in a pan and simmer gently for 1 minute. Spoon into the pancakes and fold into quarters. Sprinkle with shreds of lime rind to decorate. Serve immediately.

Cook's Tip
To freeze the crêpes, interleaf them with baking parchment and seal in a plastic bag. They should be used within 3 months.

Variation
Use strawberries instead of bananas, and orange in place of lime.

Strudel Energy 298kcal/1247kJ; Protein 4.8g; Carbohydrate 31.6g, of which sugars 18.5g; Fat 17.9g, of which saturates 5.2g; Cholesterol 18mg; Calcium 66mg; Fibre 2.4g; Sodium 55mg.
Crêpes Energy 299kcal/1263kJ; Protein 6.8g; Carbohydrate 57.2g, of which sugars 33g; Fat 6.4g, of which saturates 0.9g; Cholesterol 2mg; Calcium 125mg; Fibre 2g; Sodium 75mg.

American Spiced Pumpkin Pie

This spicy sweet pie is traditionally served at Thanksgiving in the United States and Canada, when pumpkins are plentiful.

Serves 4–6
175g/6oz/1½ cups plain
  (all-purpose) flour
pinch of salt
75g/3oz/6 tbsp unsalted butter
15g/½ oz/1 tbsp caster
  (superfine) sugar

For the filling
450g/1lb peeled fresh pumpkin,
  diced, or 400g/14oz canned
  pumpkin, drained
115g/4oz/1 cup soft light brown
  sugar
1.5ml/¼ tsp salt
1.5ml/¼ tsp allspice
2.5ml/½ tsp ground cinnamon
2.5ml/½ tsp ground ginger
2 eggs, lightly beaten
120ml/4fl oz/½ cup double
  (heavy) cream
whipped cream, to serve

1 To make the pastry, place the flour in a bowl with a pinch of salt. Rub in the butter with your fingertips until the mixture resembles breadcrumbs. Add the sugar and 30–45ml/2–3 tbsp water, then mix to a soft dough. Knead briefly, flatten into a round, wrap in cling film (plastic wrap) and chill for 1 hour.

2 Preheat the oven to 200°C/400°F/Gas 6 with a baking sheet inside the oven. If using fresh pumpkin, steam for 15 minutes, then cool. Process in a food processor or blender to form a smooth purée.

3 Line a deep pie tin (pan) with the pastry. Prick the base. Cut out leaf shapes from the excess pastry and mark veins with the back of a knife. Brush the edges with water and stick on the leaves to overlap around the pastry edge. Chill.

4 Mix together the pumpkin purée, sugar, salt, spices, eggs and cream and pour into the pastry case (pie shell).

5 Place on the preheated baking sheet and bake for 15 minutes. Then reduce the temperature to 180°C/350°F/Gas 4 and cook for a further 30 minutes, or until the filling is set and the pastry golden. Serve warm with whipped cream.

Pear & Blueberry Pie

Pears combine brilliantly with blueberries to create this popular fruit pie. It is just as delicious served cold as it is warm.

Serves 4
225g/8oz/2 cups plain
  (all-purpose) flour
pinch of salt
50g/2oz/¼ cup lard (shortening),
  diced

50g/2oz/¼ cup butter, diced
675g/1½ lb/4½ cups blueberries
25g/1oz/2 tbsp caster
  (superfine) sugar, plus extra for
  sprinkling
15ml/1 tbsp arrowroot
2 ripe but firm pears, peeled,
  cored and sliced
2.5ml/½ tsp ground cinnamon
grated rind of ½ lemon
beaten egg, to glaze
crème fraîche, to serve (optional)

1 Sift the flour and salt into a bowl. Rub in the fats with your fingertips until the mixture resembles fine breadcrumbs. Mix to a dough with 45ml/3 tbsp cold water. Chill for 30 minutes.

2 Place 225g/8oz/2 cups of the blueberries in a pan with the sugar. Cover with a lid and cook gently until the blueberries have softened. Press through a nylon sieve (strainer). Return the puréed blueberries to the pan.

3 Blend the arrowroot with 30ml/2 tbsp cold water and add to the blueberries in the pan. Bring to the boil, stirring until thickened. Allow to cool slightly.

4 Preheat the oven to 190°C/375°F/Gas 5 with a baking sheet inside the oven. Roll out just over half the pastry on a lightly floured surface and use to line a 20cm/8in shallow pie dish.

5 Mix together the remaining blueberries, the pears, ground cinnamon and lemon rind and spoon into the dish. Pour over the blueberry purée.

6 Use the remaining pastry to cover the pie. Make a slit in the centre. Brush with egg and sprinkle with caster sugar. Bake on the baking sheet for 40–45 minutes, until golden. Serve warm, with crème fraîche, if you wish.

Pumpkin Energy 411kcal/1721kJ; Protein 5.9g; Carbohydrate 47.4g, of which sugars 24.8g; Fat 23.4g, of which saturates 13.8g; Cholesterol 117mg; Calcium 96mg; Fibre 1.7g; Sodium 106mg.
Blueberry Energy 493kcal/2063kJ; Protein 7.1g; Carbohydrate 66.4g, of which sugars 23.6g; Fat 23.8g, of which saturates 11.7g; Cholesterol 38mg; Calcium 162mg; Fibre 8.6g; Sodium 84mg.

Mississippi Pecan Pie

This fabulous dessert started life in the United States but has become an international favourite.

Serves 4–6
115g/4oz/1 cup plain
  (all-purpose) flour
50g/2oz/¼ cup butter, diced
25g/1oz/2 tbsp caster
  (superfine) sugar
1 egg yolk

For the filling
175g/6oz/5 tbsp golden
  (light corn) syrup
50g/2oz/¼ cup dark muscovado
  (molasses) sugar
50g/2oz/¼ cup butter
3 eggs, lightly beaten
2.5ml/½ tsp vanilla extract
150g/5oz/1¼ cups pecan nuts
cream or ice cream, to serve

1 Place the flour in a bowl. Rub the butter into the flour with your fingertips until the mixture resembles breadcrumbs. (Alternatively use a food processor.) Stir in the sugar, egg yolk and about 30ml/2 tbsp cold water. Mix to a dough and knead on a lightly floured surface until smooth.

2 Roll out the pastry and use to line a 20cm/8in fluted loose-based flan tin (pan). Prick the base, then line with baking parchment and fill with baking beans. Chill for 30 minutes. Meanwhile, preheat the oven to 200°C/400°F/Gas 6.

3 Bake the pastry case blind for 10 minutes. Remove the paper and beans and continue to bake for 5 more minutes. Reduce the oven temperature to 180°C/350°F/Gas 4.

4 To make the filling, heat the syrup, sugar and butter in a pan until the sugar dissolves. Remove from the heat and cool slightly. Whisk in the eggs and vanilla extract and stir in the nuts. Pour into the pastry case (pie shell) and bake for 35–40 minutes, until the filling is set. Serve with cream or ice cream.

> **Variation**
> Use maple syrup instead of golden syrup.

Upside-down Apple Tart

Cox's Pippin apples are perfect to use in this classic French dessert because they hold their shape so well.

Serves 4
50g/2oz/¼ cup butter, softened
40g/1½ oz/3 tbsp caster
  (superfine) sugar
1 egg
115g/4oz/1 cup plain
  (all-purpose) flour

pinch of salt
whipped cream, to serve

For the apple layer
75g/3oz/6 tbsp butter, softened,
  plus extra for greasing
75g/3oz/scant ½ cup soft light
  brown sugar
10 eating apples, peeled, cored
  and thickly sliced

1 To make the pastry, beat together the butter and sugar until pale and creamy. Beat in the egg, then sift in the flour and salt and mix to a soft dough. Knead, wrap in cling film (plastic wrap) and chill for 1 hour.

2 For the apple layer, grease a 23cm/9in cake tin (pan), then add 50g/2oz/¼ cup of the butter. Place over low heat to melt the butter. Remove from the heat and sprinkle over 50g/2oz/¼ cup of the sugar. Arrange the apple slices on top, sprinkle with the remaining sugar and dot with the remaining butter.

3 Preheat the oven to 230°C/450°F/Gas 8. Place the cake tin on the hob again over low to medium heat for about 15 minutes, until a light golden caramel forms on the base.

4 Roll out the pastry on a lightly floured surface to around the same size as the tin and lay it on top of the apples. Tuck the pastry edges down around the sides of the apples.

5 Bake for about 20–25 minutes until the pastry is golden. Remove from the oven and leave to stand for 5 minutes.

6 Place an upturned plate on top of the tin and, holding the two together with a dish towel, turn the apple tart out on to the plate. Serve while still warm with whipped cream.

Pie Energy 373kcal/1563kJ; Protein 5.7g; Carbohydrate 51.1g, of which sugars 36.5g; Fat 17.6g, of which saturates 9.8g; Cholesterol 164mg; Calcium 59mg; Fibre 0.6g; Sodium 218mg.
Tart Energy 550kcal/2310kJ; Protein 5.4g; Carbohydrate 74.8g, of which sugars 52.9g; Fat 27.7g, of which saturates 16.7g; Cholesterol 114mg; Calcium 78mg; Fibre 4.9g; Sodium 215mg.

Index